WHAT IS
THE POINT?

WHAT IS
THE POINT?

Misty Edwards

PASSIO

Most CHARISMA HOUSE BOOK GROUP products are available at special quantity discounts for bulk purchase for sales promotions, premiums, fund-raising, and educational needs. For details, write Charisma House Book Group, 600 Rinehart Road, Lake Mary, Florida 32746, or telephone (407) 333-0600.

WHAT IS THE POINT? by Misty Edwards
Published by Passio
Charisma Media/Charisma House Book Group
600 Rinehart Road
Lake Mary, Florida 32746
www.charismahouse.com

Unless otherwise noted, all Scripture quotations are from the New King James Version of the Bible. Copyright © 1979, 1980, 1982 by Thomas Nelson, Inc., publishers. Used by permission.

Scripture quotations marked NAS are from the New American Standard Bible, copyright © 1960, 1962, 1963, 1968, 1971, 1972, 1973, 1975, 1977, 1995 by The Lockman Foundation. Used by permission. (www.Lockman.org)

Cover design by Justin Evans
Design Director: Bill Johnson

Visit the author's website at www.mistyedwards.com.

Library of Congress Control Number: 2012912454
International Standard Book Number: 978-1-61638-601-6
E-book ISBN: 978-1-62136-037-7

While the author has made every effort to provide accurate
telephone numbers and Internet addresses at the time of
publication, neither the publisher nor the author assumes
any responsibility for errors or for changes that occur after
publication.

13 14 15 16 — 9 8 7 6 5 4 3 2
Printed in the United States of America

I want to dedicate this book to my parents Robert and Donna Edwards. It would take pages to write of all that I have learned from you, but the thing I admire the most is your wholehearted devotion to Jesus and to your family. Both of you have given your lives unreservedly to love. I am moved by your radical obedience and extravagant devotion. I have rarely seen people who are so tenacious in their pursuit of God and love for people, not just for a year or two but for decades! You just don't stop, and I am eternally indebted to you for showing me the way to follow Jesus with all that I am and to love people selflessly.

I would also like thank Mike Bickle. I have heard you teach since I was a teenager and words cannot express the gratitude in my heart for all that you have given me and many others in the knowledge of God. My view of God, myself, and the world has been shaped by your wisdom, and this book is filled with truths I have learned from you. Thanks for letting us take your stuff and run with it!

To the end!

CONTENTS

FOREWORD

THIS GENERATION IS filled with "seekers." They are men and women, both old and young, who are seeking real answers and looking for the deeper meaning and purpose, not only for their individual lives but also the purpose of Creation and the whole of human history. Many of them have grown up in the church or in various religions, and others have no religious background at all, but one thing they have in common is that they feel restless in their search.

It is in the heart of all people to find the meaning of life and of death, and this search is meant to lead us directly to Jesus and His profound wisdom. One of the reasons that there is much dissatisfaction and emptiness in the hearts of even those who call themselves Christian is there is often a tragic lack of the knowledge of God and of His story. Therefore they lack of vision and purpose. People today are crying out for more than easy self-help answers to the meaning of life. They want more than to be merely propped up in their own self-pity and confusion. They want to be caught up in something bigger then themselves. There is a purpose for life and for all of human history. It is only found in the heart of the God who created everything and then gave Himself so fully to bring us to Himself. Misty Edwards says, "Until we find what God is looking for, we will never find what we are looking for." The answer to the seeking heart is found in a deeper discovery of God and His heart and plan for us.

Misty Edwards is one seeker of truth. Even as a child she could not just take what she was taught at face value but went on a persistent quest to seek for truth and real purpose behind life and history. I have watched Misty since her youth wrestle with truth and have seen her seek passionately to resolve the tensions of life and to better understand God. She is one who isn't intimidated to ask the hard questions and one who doesn't give up until she finds the answers. In this book, *What Is the Point?*, Misty gives a few of the conclusions that she has come to as a seeker of wisdom and purpose. I know Misty to be one who not only talks about truth but also seeks to live it wholeheartedly and to love Jesus with all her heart and even all her mind.

—MIKE BICKLE
DIRECTOR, INTERNATIONAL HOUSE OF PRAYER

WHY?

WHAT'S THE POINT? I'm eighteen years old, living in the middle of nowhere. Time is running out! I'm going to die one day, and I have nothing to show for my life. I'm doing nothing! Time is ticking, and I'm sitting idly by! What's the point?"

The desire for impact was like a pulse pounding in my soul. I was pacing in the hallway of our small home in Sundown, Texas, ranting and raving. There I was again in one of my frustrating outbursts that came from hours of *thinking*. My mom was in the kitchen cooking dinner, and with a sigh she was telling me to calm down.

"Calm down? How can I calm down? I'm doing nothing! I'm going to die soon, and I have nothing to show for my life? What's the purpose? What's the point? I can't calm down!"

I felt as though I were racing down a train track on a

runaway freight train while surrounded by a slow-motion film of life in Small Town, USA. I was flying through my life at a rapid pace and could already see my end in sight, but all around me people went on with business as usual, living as though we weren't going to die. I knew death was inevitable, I knew life was short, and I was desperate to find the purpose for it.

From as far back as I can remember I have been full of questions, asking why and searching for the purpose behind the "what" of life. I don't know how many times I found myself saying, "What is the point? What is the purpose of all of this?"

I grew up in a Christian home and had parents who loved the Lord. I am from a small town in Texas where the majority of the people said they were Christians and attended one of the many churches in that small community. I believed in God and had a sincere love for Jesus but could not understand Him or His reasoning behind Creation. I trusted that I was going to heaven when I died, but I could not figure out why I was alive. It wasn't a question of where I was going but why I was here. I once asked the Lord, "If the whole point of life is to get me into heaven, then why didn't You just kill me when I said the sinner's prayer and accepted Your forgiveness?" I wanted to know why I had to go through the process of life and what was the purpose of these few years I would live on the earth.

I remember multiple times sitting in the backyard on

the porch swing looking up at the vast west Texas sky and seeing the stars, feeling the impulse that is in the heart of all humans, that there is a God and He is watching. I would look up and say, "Who are You? Where are You? Are You listening? Can You see me? Why am I here?"

Even as a Christian who believed in Jesus, my mind had many questions. Often those questions were met by disapproving leaders who would tell me to "just believe," as though faith is a blind walk in the dark. This answer never satisfied my questioning but only further agitated my deep desire for understanding.

The list of my questions was long and always playing in the back of my head. I wanted to know why God was invisible. I reasoned, "If He wanted me so badly, why didn't He just stand in front of me?" Was He really that interested and that involved? I wanted to know why He created us in the first place. What was His original intention? What was the purpose of putting us in an environment where we have a proneness to sin and then giving us a sin nature that we were sure to use? Why did He let bad things happen? Why the suffering of so many in the world? Why the wealth and arrogance of others in the world who had forsaken Him without any seeming consequence? Why the boredom of life where every week seemed to repeat itself in a haunting monotony? Why the lack of passion in righteousness but a seeming invigoration in evil? Why evil at all? The devil? On and on and on my questions came almost constantly.

I drove my parents crazy with questions, and I was rarely satisfied with their answers. My heart pulsated with a deep desire for understanding and a frustration at the lack of it from those I looked to for advice. I was an agitated, melancholy seeker of the absolute with a deep desire for the truth.

I didn't want a blind faith or a trust that lacked reasoning. I couldn't just take what I was taught at face value and assume that someone had thought it through. I had to know for myself. I had to figure this thing out so that I had confidence in what I believed. I wanted life and God to make sense, and I wanted the contradictions resolved. I can honestly say that wisdom and understanding are of far more value to me than gold or silver. I wanted true faith, the kind that is backed up with evidence and substance, more than I wanted pleasure or comfort. I craved the truth. I ached for it.

EVERYBODY DIES

At the peak of my mountain of questions, the very point of the arrow, and the backbone of all that I was seeking was, "What is the purpose of life?" I believe this is the question all of us have or will have at some point in our lives, because how you answer it determines everything about you. Some people do not face this question until they are staring death in the eye. Often when someone we love dies or when we ourselves are faced with death, then we ponder the meaning of our lives. King Solomon wrote that eternity is written on the heart of man (Eccles. 3:11). I believe on the heart of every human being, no matter what religion they claim or even if they think that they are atheist, at the core of their being, thoughts of death and eternity press in on them and they wonder what the point of life is.

I heard a program on the radio talking about the fear of death. They were talking of how pervasive and powerful this fear is, and they were giving statistics saying the fear of death is the primary fear most people have. On this program they interviewed several people from all different walks of life. Those being interviewed told their stories about how petrified they were to die. Some of them would wake up in cold sweats in the middle of the night. Some could not sleep for fear that they would not wake up. Others turned to substances to try to dull the fear, and still others became depressed or irrational in their fear of death.

This program struck a chord in my heart, because as a seeker of truth I know that truth has to be found in eternity, not only in this vapor of a life. In order to find the answer to the meaning of life, we have to peer into eternity and come to conclusions on what we believe about the afterlife. What we believe about our eternal future massively defines what we believe about our momentary life.

I could relate to what King Solomon wrote in Ecclesiastes, saying that he would take his heart to the heights of humanity and imagine all that life could give him, and in the end he concluded that it's all vanity. I too would do this exercise and imagine myself in the heights of affluence only to see myself dead in the end. Maybe it was pleasure I should pursue, but still, I die in the end. Maybe I would do great humanitarian deeds and help the poor and needy, yet still, I die in the end. Everybody dies. No exceptions. It is appointed for every human to die in a very short amount of time.

All that is done "under the sun" is vanity and chasing the wind (Eccles. 1:14). It is like trying to lay hold of the wind only to come up empty-handed. It passes so quickly.

Time was ticking in my soul, and my need for answers was growing every year as life passed me by. I wanted impact. I wanted purpose. I wanted to know that whatever I was supposed to do in this life, I did with confidence. I wanted something that had continuity into eternity. There was such a sense of urgency in my soul for answers.

Like most of us, I have memories of myself at five years old trying to grasp how long forever was. All of us have tried to wrap our brains around life and death because it is written on our hearts, and the conclusions that we come to about death shape the way that we live. It's inevitable. How I answered the question of eternity defined the purpose of my life, and the question to the purpose of my life massively shaped the way I lived. But what was that answer?

DEALING WITH GOD

At nineteen I was diagnosed with cancer, and eternity pressed in on me even more. That diagnosis took my already frantic desire for relevance and purpose and catapulted me into a desperate search for the meaning of life. I had to ask, "What if I die this year? What if I die next month?" The truth is, all of us should be asking these questions right now. You should live like you are going to die, because you are going to die. I know this seems like a negative way to start a book, but let me tell you, you will die, and you don't have a lot of time to figure out what life is really all about.

In order to find meaning in life, we have to find purpose in death, and in order to face eternity, we must come to conclusions about God. You will never find sufficient meaning in a vapor called life if it is not anchored in something transcendent, with eternal continuity. In other words, to find the meaning of life we must deal with God. The purpose of life, in the most universal sense, must be accessible to all, and it must have continuity into eternity. This means we have to deal with the Creator and His original intentions in order to find the "why" behind the "what" of life. He is the only one who can make sense of this world we are in. He has the answers to why He created in the first place.

Many great thinkers throughout the ages have tried to define the meaning of life. Many of them have come to conclusions about the dignity of humans and humanity's ability to do noble things. Some have concluded that the meaning of life is pleasure. Others defined it as the choices we make to rise above any circumstance and be "good" and "triumphant." Still others have concluded the purpose is love but have stopped short of an answer that satisfies because they keep "love" defined only on human terms instead of God's. I find these theories anticlimactic and empty, because they are not addressing the fact that everybody dies—the person who loved and the person who hated dies the same. So what was the point, and where is the continuity into eternity?

Another thing that these conclusions do is define the meaning of life as nobility and love, without God at the center. If the meaning of life is found absent of God and in the goodness of humanity alone, then we are all to be pitied, because it cannot be attained or sustained.

Viktor Frankl had great insight and wrote a book called *Man's Search for Meaning*, which sold over ten million copies in twenty-four languages. But even he left me empty and incomplete. In his book he tells his own story of the great suffering he endured in World War II in Nazi prison camps. It is a moving story about the dignity of humanity, and he comes to conclusions that are profound yet incomplete.

One of his primary conclusions is that the meaning of life is for humans to use their free will, to choose how they respond to whatever fate they are given. It is the dignity of man to choose. That is the meaning of life. That is a profound conclusion, but it is only part of the truth.

If the dignity of man, to die with pride and to be a "good person," is the ultimate purpose of man and if that is the end of the story, then I am left empty and perplexed. The same fate meets the good man that meets the bad man—that fate is death. Our definitions of the meaning of life must be rooted in our conclusions about eternity, or they are less than accurate and leave us empty.

To find the purpose of life, we must find the purpose beyond the grave and come to real conclusions not only about humans but also about God. We have to get caught up in His story in order to see ours. I must admit, it is a daunting task to take on the meaning of life. I am not sufficient to define God or His story, but in my simplicity I will take the truths He has written on my heart and give them to you in order to encourage you on this same journey.

2

WHAT IS GOD LOOKING FOR?

REALIZED VERY EARLY on in my wrestling with truth and in my quest for purpose that my wrestling match was with God Himself. That mountain of questions continually led me to a face-off with God. I say that carefully, because God sits above the circle of the earth and inhabits eternity. His name is holy. He measures the ocean in the palm of His hands, and He spreads the heavens like a curtain. We cannot get rid of Him or form Him in whatever way we want to fashion Him. The universe was created and is sustained by the words of His lips (Heb. 1:3). The entire order of Creation is continuing only because He wants it to. He is God, and we have become familiar with Him and made Him in the image of what we want in "a God."

I tread with fear upon the subject of God and don't even begin to assume I have Him figured out. He is so mysterious. When I say I "wrestled with God," I say it with great reverence and fear. He doesn't owe me the answers I seek, but in His generosity and His eagerness to be known, He answers me.

The fear of the Lord is the beginning of wisdom (Prov. 9:10), and the search for purpose is the search for wisdom. We all need a greater portion of the awe of God. I am often aware of how quickly I grow dull to the sense of His majesty, but it is the foundation of all wisdom. The fear of the Lord is the root of faith. It is knowing He is really there, and He is watching. The awe of God is what enables us to feel the impact of the love of God. We see His mercy and generosity most clearly when we see His majesty and transcendence. We cannot separate the two.

If the most powerful man in the world came up to you, introduced himself, and told you he was a fan of your work or talent, the compliment would overwhelm you, right? You would take a picture, tweet it, put it on Facebook, and tell the story over and over of how that famous man loves what you do. If a random poor man came and complimented you in the same way, you would be gracious and say thank you. But maybe the impact of his compliment would hit you in a very different way. This illustrates the impact of grasping even a little about who this God is we are talking about. Do we even know whom we are dealing with when we talk about God? When our hearts get touched with an understanding of His eternal majesty, we stand in awe, and His love and mercy impact us very differently.

> The secret of the LORD is with those who fear Him, and He will show them His covenant.
> —PSALM 25:14

GOD THE CREATOR

We must look up and behold the initiator of this life and see the Creator Himself. We tremble and humbly ask Him for understanding and then search for it as a hidden treasure. It's the glory of God to hide a matter, but the one with a kingly heart will seek for it (Prov. 25:2). He is the author of life, and therefore only He has the reasoning behind it. It is utter foolishness to come up with an answer for the meaning of life outside of Him, because we were created by Him and through Him and will go to Him in the end. We were created by His will, for His pleasure (Rev. 4:11). This is why we exist and are entirely dependent upon Him.

Even the atheist is breathing only because God wills it. He is the Potter and we are the clay. Can the clay say to the Potter, "I don't like the way You are forming me, You are wrong"? Or, "I don't believe in the Potter"? It is foolish, and only a fool has said in his heart that there is no God (Ps. 14:1).

Everything in life has a cause, and everything that has order and beauty has an author or an originator. If I did not have confidence that God created the earth, I would surely just give up in despair and "eat, drink, and be merry" knowing that tomorrow I die. I cannot fathom the empty, aimless feeling of living life without God. I don't think any person is born an atheist, for even the sky itself declares God is there, and the sunrise prophesies of His goodness. The stars tell of His wonders (Ps. 19:1–6), and every man is without excuse when it comes to knowing that there is a God (Rom. 1:9).

If you are reading this and you believe in God but have a religion other than Christianity, I challenge you to take the Bible, both the Old and New Testaments, look up to the vast sky above you, and with sincerity ask God to reveal Himself to you. Then read the entire book, give God time, and I assure you, you will conclude that Jesus is God and there is no other way to life eternal. Christianity is not a blind faith; it is the wisest conclusion you can come to. I will not spend my time on this point, but I challenge you to ask for wisdom, cry out for understanding, lift up your voice, and you will find the knowledge of God (Prov. 2:3–5).

The Creator has the blueprints for life. He could have done anything He wanted, and He chose to create the human race. What was it that He was after? Some people approach God as though He were a mad scientist sitting up in heaven messing around with different potions when suddenly, poof, Creation just happened! Then humans came along and sinned, and He said, "Oh no! I didn't think about sin," as if it was all a mistake and humans made a bigger mess of God's "accident" and then He sent Jesus to clean it up, as an afterthought.

No! He has very intentionally written a story so grand—a story that we are deeply wrapped up in it. It is God's story, His own self-revelation. He has chosen the arena of humanity to make Himself known. Until we get a glimpse of that story and get caught up in the knowledge of Him, we will live aimlessly and be unable to make sense of human history. Our existence will look like history monotonously repeating itself. It will all seem irrational until we understand the story line and see that the central figure in the drama is God Himself.

He did not create, step back, and let things play out, watching from far away. He finishes what He starts, and His plan will come to pass. There is something He wants, and throughout six-thousand-plus years of human history He has been preparing humans for an end result that is beyond our comprehension. He is still actively involved and does not sit at a distance uninterested. He is looking for something, and we are moving toward something. We will not be satisfied until we satisfy Him, and we will never find what we are looking for until we find what He is looking for. Our purpose is completely defined in His.

WHAT IS HE LOOKING FOR?

What does the God who has everything want? Nothing is hidden from Him, yet He searches. What is He searching for? The Scripture makes it clear that His eyes are searching to and fro throughout the nations of the earth, looking for something (2 Chron. 16:9). He searches not only nations but also individuals from all corners of the earth, and He is peering into their hearts (1 Sam. 13:14; Rev. 2:23).

The bizarre part about His searching is that He formed the earth and the inhabitants therein, and He knows them intimately. From the edges of Creation to the core of man's thoughts, God is well acquainted with the work of His hands, yet He searches. When He designed the earth in all of its beauty and frailty, what was He thinking? When He created Adam in the garden, what was He wanting? He could have written this script in any way that He desired, and that's what He did. We are not flailing through history in randomness or monotonously spinning in space. We are on track with His desire, but what is it?

THE FREE WILL

The fact that God is eager to find something is shocking, because He is sovereign, yet in His sovereignty He designed humans with a free will. It is here that we get the first glimpse of what it is He is after.

When we are first introduced to God and His story, we see Him creating the heavens and the earth. We see Him creating man and woman in a garden. He then entrusts the earth to them, giving them dominion and authority over it (Gen. 1:26). Next we see the Lord walking in that garden with the man He created in unashamed, unhindered exchanges of thought, emotion, dialogue, and partnership.

Right from the beginning God has made His intentions known. The picture is perfect: God is walking in the garden, ruling in partnership with man. And mankind, with dominion over the earth, inhabits it in perfect harmony and beauty. There is a vibrant relationship between the Lord and the humans He entrusted the earth to. The Lord is not distant in this scene. He is near. He is right there with them in partnership and relationship. Then, there is this odd, perplexing command from God. Adam and Eve have dominion of the entire earth, but there is one tree that they cannot touch.

Immediately we see the free will at work, and instantly we recognize that God did not want only a seemingly perfect scenario; He wanted to be deliberately and personally chosen. And to be chosen, there must be a genuine free will. In this way we are created in His image. He has given us the dignity of turning from Him or turning toward Him. The one thing that He doesn't have automatically is our *volunteer* love. This is the one thing that we have to give Him, and it is the one thing that He wants. All of life comes down to the free will of man. The purpose of life is to choose to give the originator of our lives His desire.

He created mankind in His own image to have deep

fellowship with Him, yet in that same beautiful garden where He walked with them, He put the tree of the knowledge of good and evil, and in the center of that man, He put a free will. Adam, made in the image of God, had the power to choose.

The fact that we are made in God's image with the ability to choose and the capacity to have deep affections sets humans apart from all other species of life. We have severely underestimated the power of our will and the dignity that has been given to us to choose our destiny. This is the dignity and the peril of being human, and I believe it is the primary thing that God wanted in creating us.

In the garden we also see the original intention and plan of the Lord to not only have angels worship Him telling Him how beautiful He is, but He also wanted to "do something" with people. He not only wanted them to worship like the angels, but also He wanted love and relationship. He wanted to be with them, to be in partnership with them. He displayed the intention of His plan by literally entrusting the earth to them, giving dominion of it over to them. His desire for relationship and partnership was so strong that He set it up so that man could do whatever he willed with that earth, righteous or unrighteous.

This freedom to choose good or evil had to be built into the plan in order for it to be rooted in love. A love that cannot be shunned is not love at all. Without the chance and the risk of giving man a free will, there could be no true love. He already had the angels worshipping Him, but there is no indication that the angels loved Him. They do not call Him Father, and they do not call Jesus Bridegroom. (See Revelation 22:17.) They cry holy and sing of His beauty, worshipping Him both day and night, and they serve Him, but they are not in the same kind of relationship that we see the Lord had with Adam in the early days of Creation.

Very early on in the story of God we see His love was shunned as mankind operated in his free will and chose to disobey the one command he had been given, by eating of the fruit of the tree of the knowledge of good and evil (Gen. 3:1–7). Instantly a shadow was cast. The perfect scenario was gone as death entered the world and Adam and Eve were left in a wilderness.

God didn't kick Adam and Eve out of Eden just because He "got His feelings hurt" by their disobedience. Rather He had to keep them from the tree of life until the redemptive purposes had been fulfilled in Jesus (Gen. 3:24; Rev. 22:1–5). He knew from the beginning that the human story would be a process, and He was not shocked when they fell. Redemption was His plan before the foundation of the world, because He was Redeemer from eternity past. He knew that the fall of man would create the context where we would be refashioned in love. And this love would create both humility and gratitude in us that would keep us secure in giving Him our voluntary love for all eternity.

One of the primary ways of sustaining eternal, voluntary love would be through the remembrance of how much we have been forgiven. Jesus taught, "It is the one who has been forgiven much that loves much." (See Luke 7:47.) God would not violate our free will, but He ordained that we operate in it both in this age and in the age to come where we will never die. In order to secure an eternal companion for His Son, one who would love Him freely, and in order for her to be crowned with such beauty and power that she will have in the age to come, it had to be on the foundation of humility or else love would cease.

The entirety of human history is working toward God's original intention, and He is not thrown off by the process. The process of fallen humanity would further reveal the knowledge of His character and personality. He would be even better known through the story of humanity that fell away from Him, only to be purchased back by Him. We would never know His vast mercy if we did not know our vast sinfulness. We would not know Him as gracious, compassionate, slow to anger, rich in love, and delighting in mercy (Exod. 34:6) if we did not see the great divide between Him and us that was caused by our sin. Without the forgiveness of sin in the story, we would not have gratitude, and much of what we know about God would be left unknown. It is all working to reveal God, and we are wrapped up in His story. The human story tells God's story, and the purpose of humanity, as a whole, is to reveal the knowledge of God. It is here that we find meaning and purpose for our lives. His story is stunning, and we must get caught up in it if we are ever going to understand humanity and our own individual lives.

OLD TESTAMENT

As the story of God continued, the Lord made His will known, drawing men to His creative purpose and their original design. Over and over He beckoned them to become what they were created to be, and when they refused and chose sin, it caused "distortion" and "unrighteous." This is where the tension of life comes in as we see the struggle between God and man. When men refuse to come into agreement with the Creator, it is a "distortion" and it is not right. He cannot let it go on and on with men refusing Him, because the earth itself cannot bear this refusal and mankind cannot survive under this refusal.

His plan would have been be lost if He didn't address the rebellion of man. The Creator is not going to miss the mark and come up short of what He originally wanted. Love is a two-sided coin, and He is jealous and exclusive—not because He is insecure, but because, by design, we are fashioned for Him. When we turn from Him to humanism, secularism, or any other religion, we become distorted and it leads to our destruction. He loves us too much to let that happen, so He often will create a scenario that makes us run back to Him. Even His chastisements are about His primary motivation, which is to have relationship with humans, in partnership and love (Heb. 12:6).

Throughout the centuries God has not been silent as men have accused. He has not been disinterested or even hard to figure out. He has been shouting, and even creation itself has been telling us who He is, what He is like, and what He desires. Yet in the midst of the Creator's vehement pleas and loud beckoning, so few will ever respond and look back at Him.

This is the mystery, not of how hidden God is, but of how quickly we tune Him out. We are like children with our fingers in our ears screaming loudly with our eyes tightly shut, "I can't see You! I can't hear You! Where are You?" All the while He is right in front of us, if we will just open our eyes and ears and respond.

Of the billions of people on earth throughout history the majority have refused Jesus. They have denied heaven's pleas and have shut their ears to their own heart's cry for a purpose that is eternal. They have chosen to live in the delusion of today, or they have turned to other gods in an attempt to appease their questions of death and life without being held responsible to the true God.

We see that this is the tension that rose to a boiling point throughout the Old Testament. By the time we get to the end of the Book of Malachi, we are left wondering what will happen to God's plan. It seems to us, at this point in the story, that humans will never choose Him in a consistent way. It seems His beauty is not sufficient to draw them or His judgments not severe enough to convince them to return to Him and stay with Him. Yet again God is not thrown off. It's all working.

THE LOGOS

During the first four-thousand-plus years of human history God was telling His story, and little by little He was giving hints of His personality. He spoke in the poetry of nature, in the riddles of prophecy, and on the canvas of Israel, but all of it was culminating to a point in history where He Himself would step into the canvas and declare Himself openly. He spoke through the patriarchs, He spoke through the prophets, He spoke through the men of old, and then the great artist of life stepped onto the canvas and took on the form of man in order to speak plainly in the language men can understand. He Himself came to plead with us. (See Matthew 21:33–43.)

I heard David Pawson, one of the most well-known and respected Bible teachers in the United Kingdom, give a teaching once on Jesus being the Word of God. He said something that really struck a chord in my heart, as a seeker of purpose. He said:

> When John wrote his Gospel after knowing Jesus for sixty years, he had a problem: What do you call Jesus before He was born? He thought up a brilliant answer, and in Greek he called Him *Logos*. Among other meanings, this means,

"Word." He called Him "the Word." In the beginning was the Word and the Word was with God, face-to-face, and the Word was God. He is writing, "In the beginning was the Word." Why did he choose that? Because in Ephesus there was a Greek scientist called Heraclitus who invented science, and he taught his students to observe and analyze and said, "Try and find the reason why nature behaves like it does. Study nature and animals and try and find the reason why it happens like it does." He called the reason why *ho logos*, so all science is called an "-ology," trying to find the reason why.

Science is dedicated to finding *ho logos*, and in choosing that word as the name of preexistent Jesus, he [John] is saying, "He is the supreme reason why."

...Science becomes more specialized and knows more and more about less and less, but scientists don't stop to ask, "What is the reason of the whole of nature operates like it does? Why is it all here?" John is saying, "Jesus is why it is all here. God made it all for Jesus, and He will inherit it all," and we shall inherit it with Him. The meek inherit the earth. He is the reason why. I love that title...Jesus is the reason why everything happens as it does.

Logos—oh! How I love this title for Jesus! The purpose of Creation is Jesus! The beginning of life is Jesus; the purpose of life is Jesus; the meaning of life and the ending of life is Jesus. He is God, and it is His story we are wrapped up in. Creation itself was made for Him, and He will inherit all of it (Col. 1:16). Jesus is the reason we exist. Jesus is the purpose of our lives. He is the beginning, middle, and end.

Jesus is not a hippie, laid back and hanging out without a vision. He isn't some kind of guru who walked around barefooted and passive. No, He is God. He is the one who appeared in the burning bush before Moses. He's the one who shook Mount Sinai causing the children of Israel to be terrified and to beg Moses to talk to Him for them. He's the same one who caused both the temple structure and the prophet Isaiah to shake before Him (Isa. 6; John 12:41). He's the same one Ezekiel saw in that great vision he had of God as a whirlwind of raging fire. In the midst of that whirlwind, he saw the Man who is fully God yet fully man (Ezek. 1:26). He saw Jesus and trembled in awe. He could not believe His eyes. This is the same Man whom John the beloved fell in front of like a dead man when He appeared to him in His full glory (Rev. 1:17). This is the same God who hung the stars in space, who numbered the hairs of your head, and who is upholding you by the word of His mouth (Heb. 1:3). Let us not forget who we are talking about when we so flippantly say the name "Jesus."

If you do not believe Jesus is God, you will spend your life searching for purpose and come up empty. I challenge you, even now, to ask Him to reveal Himself to you, then wait and see what He will do. Many men have tried to define life's meaning outside of Jesus, and all their attempts have ended in futility and vanity.

There is no ultimate, lasting purpose outside of Him. There is no eternal meaning for life and death outside of Jesus, because He is God. He is the author of our lives, and only He has the right to define us. We will never be content until we are what He intended us to be. He designed us for Himself, and until we are fully His, we will feel off balance, uncentered, empty, and aimless. Our life is wrapped in Him, and only when we see Him, do we ever see ourselves. By beholding Him, we become like Him, therefore fulfilling our primary life purpose.

AT FIRST GLIMPSE

I was eighteen when I first began to catch a glimpse of Jesus's story and get caught up in the bigger picture of what He wanted and what He was looking for. I had decided that the only hope of finding purpose in this life was to find purpose in death, and the only answers to life after death were my conclusions about eternity and God. I became preoccupied with knowing God and trying to understand His ways. I knew that until I settled what I believed about God, I would never fulfill my purpose in life because everything outside of Him was temporary and fragile. I started to read the Bible and ask questions. I tried to learn to pray and to fast as a means to know Him. I was not good at any of these things.

I remember being in my bedroom, reading the Book of Exodus, wondering why Jesus wouldn't just show up and talk to me face-to-face as He did with Moses. I thought, "This would be so much easier if You would just sit here in front of me and have a conversation." The invisibleness of God was the big argument I had with Him.

I realize it is presumptuous for me to ask for a face-to-face encounter, but I think He smiled on my youthful zeal that dared ask the Genesis 1 God to stand in front of me!

Prayer was hard, the Bible was mostly boring, and I didn't understand fasting. I would try to pray but couldn't figure out how to sustain it. I tried to read the Bible but found myself distracted. He was smiling on me all the while though, and He was calling my heart to Himself.

At nineteen I decided to move to Kansas City and attend a Bible school there. My idea was to move to Kansas City, go to Bible school for a year, learn the Bible, and gain understanding on how God communicates with people today. I wanted to know Him, and I wanted that to be my supreme purpose. I knew everything else in life would flow from this fountain.

I was fresh away from home, tenacious for truth, longing for God, working hard, and never sleeping. It was a good year and a trying one. In the midst of all of this, I was experiencing severe pain in my right leg because of a tumor that was growing in the nerve of my leg. I was in so much pain that I rarely slept. Like most college-aged kids, I was up late and awake early. I was in a whirlwind of activity with this nagging hunger for truth, though I did not have time to satisfy it.

Jesus's leadership is perfect, and He is kind in the way He woos us to Himself. All of these years later, I look back on that time of my life with tears of gratitude. I had joined Bible school in order to "know God." I moved away from home and came to a place rich in understanding. But in the midst of my pursuit, I became so busy, social, and frenzied that my faith was weakened instead of growing deeper.

I thought Bible school was the answer to my questions, but I could not get the impact of much of the truth I was learning. However, I was growing in understanding, though it was small and seemed insignificant. I was moving forward little by little. In a way I did not fully grasp, I was growing in faith as my paradigm of Jesus was slowly changing.

The one class that marked me the most that fall was the class Mike Bickle taught on the Song of Solomon. I had never heard such magnificent truths about the purpose of Creation. I had never heard Jesus desired relationship with humanity, even in our weakness. Mike also talked about the longings of the human heart that God put in us, and how those longings cannot be repented of but they are escorts into God's heart and into the supreme story of God and humanity. He talked about our desire for meaning and purpose and how it is primarily found in Jesus. It was as though the strings of my heart were being played, and I was being beckoned into a great mystery. I was still on a swinging pendulum between faith and unbelief, but something about the truths in this class drew me like a magnetic force into the divine story of God Himself.

I wasn't able to grasp all that was being said. I was too busy and chaotic. But like everything in life in God, a seed had been planted that would one day blossom and bear fruit. I did not realize, at the time, the impact that this class was having on me, but the seeds were taking root.

During those months of being so social and scattered, living the student life, I would sneak away to the laundry room in the basement of the apartment building I lived in. It was the only place I could ever find privacy. I would sit in that basement, with its concrete floors and cobwebs, reading the Song of Solomon commentary. I would also read through the Bible, especially reading the scriptures pointing to what God is searching for. I would look out the small, dingy window near the ceiling of those dirty walls into the dark, star-filled sky and pray to the Invisible, "Is this true? Is this really how You feel? Do You have this kind of passion for me? Are You really watching me? Is all of creation about loving Jesus?" I knew if this story was real, it changed everything for me. If the story was true, then I would do anything and live any way in order to feel the impact of it. I wept in longing. I wanted it to be true. I hoped it was true, and in my foggy belief I reached out to lay hold of His heart, even as He was laying hold of mine.

Though these laundry room moments were precious to me, they were not enough to keep me from distraction during that semester. The lack of sleep because of the growing tumor in my leg, the proneness to too much social life, long hangouts, drinking coffee, and early mornings teaching three-year-olds made for a chaotic person when I went home for the holidays that year. Though frazzled and still full of questions, I was changing. Faith was working in me, though it seemed small and slow. That Song of Solomon class had made an undeniable impact on me, and something was pulling my heart that made me want to draw away and be with the Lord. I wanted to sit at my piano and sing to Him. I wanted to lock my door and pray to Him.

FINDING MEANING IN THE MIDST OF PAIN

I went home for the Thanksgiving, and while I was there, I decided it was time to see a doctor about the pain in my leg. Little did I know that doctor appointment would keep me in Texas for several months, and I would not be returning to Kansas City as planned. It was at this time I was diagnosed with cancer. The doctor was shocked at the size of the tumor that was growing in my nerve and immediately scheduled an operation.

I spent that Thanksgiving in the hospital in Dallas. The doctors did not know if it was malignant or not, and they were not sure if they could remove the tumor and save my leg. There were talks of amputation or a lifelong foot brace, and there was much worry about the tumor spreading and possibly costing me my life. My world was changing in a matter of weeks as I stood at the mountain of my familiar ponderings on death and life.

Being nineteen years old and having cancer put me on an even faster pace in coming to conclusions about the purpose of life. I went through a couple surgeries and a round of chemotherapy that winter. I lost my hair around Christmas and became weak with the drugs that were meant to kill the remaining tumor. I can honestly say, this was one of the best times in my life. I do not believe God gave me cancer, and I believe in supernatural healing. I fought against sickness throughout this entire season, yet God drew me to Himself in the process.

The story of God I had heard through the Song of Solomon class was so fresh on my heart that I felt carried throughout this season. If the story was real, I had nothing to lose. I felt I was coming into the knowledge of my purpose in life and truly felt a grace on my heart that, looking back, was supernatural. Because I was sick for those few months, I had much time to sit, reflect, sing, write, and be with the Lord. I felt His presence strong as I thought about eternity and life. It was a sweet three months, even though I was in and out of the hospital.

It all seemed small to me. If Jesus really felt about me the way that was described in the Bible, and if He was literally watching my heart, then I had it made and I had nothing to fear.

There was more to life than meets the eye, more to life than only pursuing the American dream, more to life than physical beauty, and even more to life than health and happiness. Eternity was being written on my heart, and I wouldn't trade it for the world.

Viktor Frankl wrote in *Man's Search for Ultimate Meaning* that "despair is suffering without meaning."[1] We can go through anything in life if we know that it has meaning. This became more and more true to me as I asked questions about suffering and death, even as a teenager seeking truth. My conclusions about the purpose of life were growing stronger, though I did not have the full application for them. Something was happening in me where my life dream was changing, and the perspective from where I lived that dreaming was changing as well. Even though my faith was small, it was growing.

Our definition of the meaning of life must transcend all life circumstances in order for it to be real. When I was healthy and feeling great or sick and in the hospital, I had purpose. If I had ninety years or nine months to live, the purpose of life had to be attainable in every circumstance. The ultimate meaning of human existence must be available to all, no matter their social status, education, health, beauty, or nationality, or else the Creator is not just. The purpose for which we were created is attainable by all who want it.

During these months of fighting with cancer, when my future was so uncertain, I could still fulfill the will of God for my life and have meaning and purpose. My definition of life began to change. I was still climbing that mountain of questions and still found my heart agitated at moments, trying to grapple with meaning and truth. In my youth I was like a swinging pendulum, going from contentment before God and having faith in Him to the opposite extreme of unbelief and frustration. But through these extremes my heart was becoming strong in my convictions.

When I see someone asking hard questions and fighting for answers, or when I see a person struggling with God, I don't interrupt their struggle or tell them to get over it. God is not offended by our questions, and He is not nervous about our mind swinging like a pendulum. When we ask, in sincerity, without accusation, He leads us into truth. He wants to give us answers that are written on our hearts so that in the hour of the real shaking, we won't move. It is healthy and good for a person to fight for truth and not to just believe what they are told. I will tell people what I have learned and boldly declare the truth of Jesus to those on their way to hell, but I will not interrupt the wrestling match of a sincere believer who is wrestling to know Jesus's name for themselves. I look back over the years and see how many marvelous conclusions I came to in one season of my life only to doubt them in the next. And then I would work it out and end up in a deeper conviction after the whole exercise was done.

This is the way that truth gets written on your heart and what you really believe about life and God gets set in stone. The seasons of life test your beliefs, and it is good and healthy to ask questions without fear. Truth is the stone on which the soul chisels. At every stage you think you know what you are concluding and you think you have the sculpture as a finished product, only to find that it's not quite right. The soul who seeks continues to chisels away at the stone of truth until it is formed with beauty and unshakable conclusions.

I had survived one battle with cancer and was changed because of it. I had a new measure of resolve to please Jesus as the supreme meaning of my life. I continued to climb my mountain of questions as I returned to Kansas City, a calmer and more focused person.

3

BEFORE HIS EYES

THROUGHOUT OUR LIVES the desire for purpose comes up again and again, no matter what initially drives us. This is because of the power and the gift of disillusionment. Though disillusionment implies disappointment, it is a gift when it leads us to the truth. There are two things in life that lead us to our eternal purpose: pain or the fulfillment of pleasure. When what drives us is not eternal purpose but temporal accomplishment, we eventually face the end of it. Then when it is attained, it is disappointing or over so quickly that we are left with sadness because the dream that was driving us is no longer in front of us. Sometimes we feel aimless when we attain what once motivated us or we live in pain because we cannot get what we dream of.

I heard a famous movie star being interviewed. The host was asking him how it felt to finally make it in the movies after dreaming about it from the time he was a child. The interviewer went on with the questioning, asking how it felt to come through all of the trials in life he had to overcome in order to get to his dream. Everyone applauded the greatness of humanity demonstrated in how someone could overcome so much, then "arrive," and become what they had always dreamed of becoming. The actor then surprised everyone with his answer: "It's boring." He said, "My whole life I dreamt of doing films, and now I find it's boring."

I could hear the near appalling disillusionment in his voice. He was shocked that the thing that had driven him and shaped him left him empty when he attained it. The stories go on and on of people who have been motivated by a temporary dream, only to attain it and then feel empty and aimless. Many others never attain their earthly dream, and they live in great pain over it. Their entire lives they dream of becoming something, and when they cannot get it, they are in agony and feel like failures.

Our primary purpose in life must exceed temporary attainments, goals, and dreams. There must be a dream that is unbreakable and inexhaustible, yet attainable. It is a dream that is transcendent and makes us who possess it people the world rarely sees or understands. We become like strangers or pilgrims in this life, pressing on toward a goal that is progressively attained and eternally expanding. We must have an untouchable dream that will not be fully attained in this life in order to find eternal meaning.

Because time is motion and life continually moves forward, toward something, we must have something in front of us, else we will be aimless—and aimlessness leads to despair.

The law of time cannot changed, and time demands we move forward. This means that the purpose of life must be rooted in something that moves forward and is so vast that it has no end. An unending goal that is attained a little at a time will be the life dream that sustains you both now and forever.

AUDIENCE OF ONE

This dream is found in the eyes of the "Audience of One." In our quest for meaning we must find it in Jesus's eyes, confident that He is watching us and that what we do matters, because it is before Him and not before the changing opinion of man.

Men love you one minute and ridicule you the next. One year you're cool, and the next you're outdated and old. One season you are successful, and the next you are a failure. This is true in finances, relationships, ministry, impact, influence; everything in life is on a quick fade.

We cannot anchor our desire for meaning in these things, because it would be like chasing the wind. Though these things are important and relevant, they are secondary and not the anchor of our lives. When we live before His eyes and seek to be pleasing to Him, above all else, then everything we do in life has meaning and eternal significance. We will live knowing He sees, remembers, and rewards. This is the power of our lives.

Everybody Dies

> It is appointed for men to die once, but after this, the judgment.
>
> —Hebrews 9:27

Everybody dies. There's no way around it. When we die, we will stand before our Creator at the judgment seat of Christ (2 Cor. 5:10). This is the place where we are evaluated and rewarded by Jesus in the age to come. It is a picture similar to the top athletes standing at the Olympic podium where the medals are given. It is appointed that at the end we stand before the author of our lives. Only He can tell us we "hit the mark." He is able to be the evaluator of our lives, because He is the Creator, the one who holds the blueprints of humanity. Only He has the standard by which we can be measured. He is also a man who walked on the earth, showing us how to be human. He was tested in all the ways we are and is acquainted with our suffering (Heb. 4:15). He is fully God and fully man, the only person who can judge us in perfect justice and truth. We cannot evaluate one another and conclude that we are successful or not.

The greatest appointment of my life is yet in the future. It is the day I stand before Jesus, the great evaluator of my life. I will stand before one man, and I will have a conversation. My entire life comes down to what He thinks about me. My entire purpose lies in pleasing Him (2 Cor. 5:9–10).

Life is a vapor; it passes quickly like the steam from a boiling pot. At best we have seventy to one hundred years, but we are not even guaranteed that long to prepare for the one conversation that matters most. There is only one appointment where we are told whether our lives were wasted or if we fulfilled our purpose. It doesn't make sense to ignore the one man we will stand before who has the full power to evaluate our lives. It makes no sense to ignore that or to pretend and assume that day will just somehow go away. It will not go away. None of us will miss that appointment. We may miss many appointments, but we will not miss that one, I assure you.

Jesus is not only truthful, but also He is truth (John 14:6). When we are in the presence of truth incarnate, the truth about us will come to the light. It is impossible to trick Jesus or to be fake and unauthentic before His eyes. He sees right through all of our rhetoric, religiosity, and manipulation. You cannot convince Him you are something you are not. He sees and He knows.

I am not interested in what men define as the meaning of life. All that matters is how Jesus defines purpose. If the entire world applauded me, thought I was noble, and praised me saying I was a picture of what a human should be, it would mean nothing, absolutely nothing, if Jesus did not agree. When I stand before Jesus, it will be just

Him and me. No one will be there to tell Him how great I am, how many records I sold, or the numbers of people I impacted. No one will be there to tell Him how bad I am and the sins I have committed. In that day what is true will be seen.

The most important thing about my life is what Jesus is thinking. Whatever He is thinking, in that moment I stand before Him, is the most important thing about my life, even right now. When I stand before the Lord, He is going to ask me about how big my heart was in responsiveness to Him. That is what matters.

OUR AMBITION TO PLEASE HIM

The apostle Paul was preoccupied with Jesus's evaluation of him. It is what drove Paul and motivated him to run the race with endurance. This is also what should make us unwavering in every life circumstance.

In 2 Corinthians 5:9 Paul said, "We also have as our ambition...to be pleasing to Him" (NAS). We want Him pleased because He is Creator. We were created for His pleasure, and we will never be satisfied until we satisfy Him. He is also judge, and we want to please Him because only He can evaluate the worth of our lives and therefore give us meaning. We are motivated by worth.

The greatest fear I have is to be worthless. To have no purpose and meaning is the absolute terror of my life. My worth is found in Jesus's eyes and in His evaluation of me. My worth is defined there and there alone.

Paul said it clearly, "We make it our aim...to be well-pleasing to Him." There was a moment in Paul's life where he consciously determined this would be the primary dream of his life. He determined this would be the supreme preoccupation of his life, walking with the Lord and living his entire life to be well pleasing to Him. To "make it his aim" means it is the primary reason for why he had life on the earth. He is not saying, "I made this one of my top ten things on my to-do list." No, this was the primary ambition of his life.

We have many dreams in our heart that are biblical and of God. We have dreams related to ministry, money, marriage, health, and impacting others. We have dreams and promises related to these very important subjects. They are biblical, and they are important to God, but they must be of secondary importance to this one, primary aim.

Nobody can make this your aim. It must be your choice. This is why it is powerful to the heart of God, because it is voluntary, and therefore it is love. You can be saved without setting your heart to live in extravagance before His eyes. There are many people who know Jesus as Savior and will be in heaven, but they lived their lives without giving much further thought to Him. They are saved and please Him in the sense that they have the free gift of righteousness, but there is another element of pleasing Him that comes when we set our hearts to live wholeheartedly before Him. This is what Paul was talking about. Once you determine this is your primary life dream, if you are like me, you have to make it your aim and reestablish it, realigning yourself over and over again.

I will realign myself to this many more times, because it is the nature of our weakness to get disoriented and distracted from this aim. Over and over I stop and realign my heart to make this the primary ambition of my life. It is the unbreakable dream. When you picture your future, don't just picture yourself in love with a happy family, lots of money, and lots of friends—the typical American dream. These are good things, but there is more to your life than this. When you think of twenty or thirty years from now, do you have a dream to be walking in a way, in both heart and action, that is pleasing in God's sight? Do you know what it is to please Him, and have you determined in your heart to do it? This is the primary picture you should have of your life when you think about your future. Yes, money, relationships, family, and ministry are valid desires in the will of God, but there is a bigger definition of success that is beyond these things.

We Are Well Known to the Lord

> Knowing, therefore, the terror of the Lord, we persuade men; but we are well known to God.
> —2 Corinthians 5:11

Paul not only understood he had a great appointment; he also understood that the judge, the one evaluating him, was deeply invested and engaged with the details of his life. If we know Jesus is engaged and cares about the efforts we are making that nobody else cares about...if we know He sees the small acts of obedience...if we believe we are well known to Him, that He really cares about these things and remembers them, writes them in His books and rewards us forever, then our lives change. If we know we have an appointment to stand before our Creator and the Creator Himself knows even the intricacies of our lives and what we do matters to Him, then we have purpose. Jesus is the One who searches the heart and the mind (Rev. 2:23).

King David said God fashioned our hearts individually and He considers our works (Ps. 33:15). This means He sees what we are doing and actually thinks about it and ponders it. David also wrote of how God searched him and knew him (Ps. 139:1). This was the power driving David's life. Like Paul, he knew God knew him well and was paying attention. This is a stunning reality to those who believe it.

THE GREAT EQUALIZER

The exciting thing is no matter the size of your natural talents or your station in life, the judgment seat of Christ is the great equalizer, because our responsiveness to God is what He measures us by. He does not measure how big your ministry is or how big your bank account is. He doesn't even measure how many people you are able to impact. He measures the size of your heart. This is the true measure of a man.

Someone could be far more gifted and impact many more people than you, but if your responsiveness is the same, you get the same reward. To be rewarded means there is an appointed day in history when Jesus wants to communicate openly to you, and to others, how He feels about the way you loved Him. He wants to express it openly.

What a tragedy it would be on that day for Him to have little to say about the way I lived on the earth. When we have the confidence that He is attentive and remembers even the smallest words spoken and rewards the smallest reach toward Him, this is faith. When we believe Jesus, as Creator, is this attentive and this eager, we will want to please Him. Our purpose is found in His eyes.

LOCKED GAZE

I remember when this "locked gaze" became a living reality to me. After a yearlong battle with cancer and a lifelong wrestle with truth, I was more determined than ever to figure out what Jesus wanted from me. I was more aware than ever that life was short and I would die and face Him soon. I became consumed with thoughts of eternity, and small things became small while big things became big. My entire worldview started to change as I pondered eternity, the frailty of life, and the day that I would stand in front of Jesus for His evaluation of me.

It was at this time that the International House of Prayer in Kansas City, Missouri, started. I was one of the first interns, and I jumped right into day and night prayer, because I was eager to know God. I felt this was the ideal environment for me to pursue Him. Words are not sufficient to describe the transformation that took place in me as I stood before the Lord day and night. IHOP-KC was small, and we were keeping perpetual prayer with worship going in these small trailers with only a handful of people. It seemed really weak and fragile, yet it was where I found the gaze of Jesus.

Formed and fashioned in the early days of the house of prayer, I did not consider myself a real singer or musician. I knew only a few chords on the piano and only a few songs. Yet because prayer and worship had to go on continually twenty-four hours a day, seven days a week, I could not stop. I ended up singing and leading for six or eight hours in a day. I would sing for two hours, sit down and read the Bible for two hours, then sing again.

The prayer room was mostly empty, and the music was mostly bad. It seemed small and insignificant. I also cleaned the building as part of my job, and I was the "copy girl" who made copies for everyone. I would clean and make copies, then go back to singing and reading. This was my life for the first few years of IHOP-KC, and I worked the muscle of faith over and over and over. I knew this was the will of God for my life at that time.

There were times I felt like I was wasting my life, but

I knew I was in His will. I cannot tell you how many times I asked myself, "Why are you doing this? Sitting in a room, telling God what He tells you to tell Him? You are wasting your time. What are you doing? You could have changed the world. You could have done great things. Why are you sitting in a room talking to an invisible person?"

Again and again I would have this dialogue with myself. I would answer my frantic fear of wasting my life by telling myself that He was watching me and that this is what He had asked me to do at this time in my life. So day and night I would offer my gaze back to Him, even though it was through a dim glass and at times it was shaky.

Over time faith grew in my heart. I was coming in contact with God. For the first time in my life I was really interacting with Him and knowing Him experientially, as well as knowing Him through the renewing of my mind. My inner man was being recoded as my desires were changing, and I was being transformed into His image the more I beheld Him (2 Cor. 3:18). I was so weak, and I failed often. There were times I was bored and irritated that I had so much to offer God and all He had asked me to do was pray and serve. I thought, "I could have changed the world, but You want me to sit here and tell You what You already know?" It was not always easy, and there wasn't perpetual bliss, but little by little my cold heart was melting and the seeds of faith were growing as my perspective of God and life started to change. I was transferring my primary life dream from what I could do to what I wanted to become. I was changing what drove me from impact to intimacy, and I was getting caught up in a burning desire to please Him as the primary purpose of my life. I definitely do not think it is God's will for everyone to join a day and night prayer ministry, but it is His will for everyone to live before His eyes.

We all feel as if we are wasting our lives at times, but when we know we are in His will and He is pleased with us, we have power in our hearts. He is watching and it counts. Life is not in vain. When we know we exist for His pleasure and we will never be satisfied until we satisfy Him, we become preoccupied with pleasing Him.

We are motivated by both pleasure and fear. When we realize that life is short and there is a judgment day on which we will stand before one man and His opinion is all that matters, it profoundly motivates us to please the one who judges. Both the pleasure of pleasing Him and the fear of coming up short keep us locked into His eyes. Even though we fail many times, we return again and again to that locked, steady gaze.

The apostle Paul's dream was unbreakable. He could be in prison, he could be in front of a multitude, or he could be suffering great persecution. Still Paul had a deep desire to be pleasing in Jesus's sight, and he kept his eyes on this prize knowing that wisdom would be justified (Matt. 11:19). It was his primary goal, and he often spoke of it and wrote about it. This was the dream that kept him steady through persecution and promotion. He counted it all as loss—the good and the bad. This desire to be pleasing in Jesus's sight creates humility and steadfastness in a man.

> Not that I have already attained, or am already perfected; but I press on, that I may lay hold of that for which Christ Jesus has also laid hold of me. Brethren, I do not count myself to have apprehended; but one thing I do, forgetting those things which are behind and reaching forward to those things which are ahead, I press toward the goal for the prize of the upward call of God in Christ Jesus.
>
> —PHILIPPIANS 3:12–14

ANYBODY CAN DO IT

A person who lives before Jesus's eyes, determined to give Him what He is looking for, is able to become eternally great no matter what this life has given him (Matt. 5:19). This is true liberation. No one can touch a man or a woman who lives like this. Their money can be taken, they can lose relationships and positions, and they can be thrown into prison, persecuted, or even martyred. Still they will attain what they are aiming for. A person can be uneducated and unattractive, sitting on the back row where nobody notices them. This person has the same capacity to be as eternally great in God's eyes as the person who is the most educated, beautiful, and seemingly successful in the eyes of man today.

God does not measure us as men measure us. Paul knew this. Church history is full of men and women who were free because they lived before Jesus's eyes even when they were thrown into prison for their faith. History proves that living before the eternal eyes is the power and worth of a person, and anyone and everyone can do it. I love Jesus's ways! Anybody, everybody, who wants to be eternally great can be, and we are not at the mercy of the rise and fall of external favor and blessing. Our definition of greatness is not affected by our assignment in life. We have assignments that are important, and we serve in these assignments with faithfulness, but the measure of success in these arenas is not in our hands. We cannot build our confidence on them. Our confidence is in serving in our assignment before the Audience of One.

The issue is whose applause we are living for. We may do the same assignment, but the Lord wants us to readjust our hearts. People do not burn out because their assignment is too difficult. They burn out because they are doing their assignment before the wrong set of eyes, looking for the wrong applause. The heart is often revealed when we are criticized. If we are thrown off by criticism, we are living before the wrong eyes.

Failure is another test. When our life assignments seem to fail—we lose money, our ministries shrink, or our relationships fail—of course we feel the pain. But if we are devastated by these things, concluding our whole life is a failure because of them, it is proof we are not living before the Audience of One. We are living for the applause of man. Many times Jesus will test our hearts in this way to show us where our true value lies. We realign ourselves again and again to live before His eyes.

MIKE

I have often heard Mike Bickle talk about his primary definition of success and greatness is to be well pleasing to Jesus. He has made it his aim to live before the Audience of One, knowing that he will be evaluated by the measure of his heart responses to Jesus.

He tells the story of the International House of Prayer in Kansas City. There was a sign on his wall in the church prayer room, prophesying about the House of Prayer that would one day go nonstop twenty-four hours a day, seven days a week, with singers and musicians. For about fifteen years before it actually started, people would ask him what it meant, and he would say, "It's something we will do some day."

Then the time came for IHOP-KC to start, and people would come up to him and say, "You did it! You have your dream!" He would answer them by saying, "IHOP-KC is not my dream. It is my assignment. My dream is to go somewhere in God and to live before His eyes, pleasing Him." He says, "IHOP-KC can grow and be successful in the eyes of man or it can get smaller and be unsuccessful in the eyes of man. Either way my dream is not affected because my dream is to touch the heart of Jesus and be pleasing in His sight, not to build a big ministry. This is my assignment, not my dream."

Our assignments are important, but we are not meant to find our primary identity or purpose in them.

PAT

The story that moves me the most is that of Pat Bickle, Mike's brother. He was paralyzed from the neck down after an injury he suffered while playing football in high school. Toward the end of Pat's life, after being paralyzed for thirty-three years, he got very ill and ended up unable to speak or even drink water. His mind was alert, and he was the same man he had been his entire life, full of wit and love for people, but he could not communicate. For weeks he lay like this.

In the meantime Mike's ministry was growing and thousands of young people were coming to his conferences. He had traveled the world preaching. He had written books, taught thousands, and impacted many people.

As Pat lay there in the last few weeks of his life, Mike went to see him almost daily. On one of these days it was just Mike and Pat in the hospital room. Mike looked at Pat as he lay there, suffering more than most humans ever suffer, unable to speak, move, or drink. He said, "Pat, right now today, you can fulfill the will of Jesus for your life as much as I can. His will for you today is that you love Him without offense and that you believe He is watching you even now. You can please Him and touch His heart as much as I can today. He sees your love for Him as much as He sees mine."

Tears were streaming down Pat's face as he dared to believe that even in suffering, he could do God's will even if it meant just loving Him in that horrible situation. These months in his life were not in vain. There was a purpose for his life, even in that place of great suffering. Jesus was watching him and promised to reward him for every movement of his heart. Pat can be eternally great as much as his famous brother can be, because Jesus evaluates us based on our heart responses to Him and our love for Him, not on the size of our ministry or business impact.

HE SEES YOU

This primary purpose of our lives to please Jesus must become our compulsion and our consuming dream. We want to be preoccupied with Jesus and less occupied with the opinion of man. This is the prize that is set before us, and it must be the anchor of our souls. Nothing can take this dream away from you when it is your primary motivation, and it can be attained no matter what life circumstance you are in.

It doesn't matter what sphere you have been given. You could be on the backside of nowhere and have only two or three people who are listening to you, or you could be on a stage in front of millions. You could be healthy, full of charisma and charm, so that people naturally follow you, or you could be ill and unable to communicate clearly. You can be rich or poor, beautiful or not. You can be educated or uneducated, from any nationality, any social background and still fulfill the vision Jesus has for you and therefore be eternally great and successful at fulfilling your life purpose.

Eternity is the great equalizer, and the true measure of a man is found in Jesus's eyes. You can have the hardest past, full of abuse and pain, or you could be the one who caused others pain by abusing, yet you can still today turn things around and fulfill the dream of His heart for your life and live with confidence that your life is not in vain.

You may never be great in the eyes of man. You may live your whole life overlooked, but there is one man who sees, and He is so attentive to you that He knows your thoughts and your deepest emotions (1 Cor. 4:5). He sees all and judges all, and His evaluation is what matters. You will be standing in front of Him, face-to-face, in a very short amount time, and His evaluation of you will be what defines you for billions of years.

This makes life today powerful. Not only is there a Man who is fully God who is attentive to you, but also He promises to reward you. Every act of love you give Him will be rewarded in the age to come, and only then will the truth about you be seen.

Your life is hidden, and you will not appear until He appears in glory. The fullness of your greatness is hidden even from your own eyes in this age, and it will not be revealed, even to you, until Jesus is revealed (Col. 3:3–4). You do not see the heights of your dignity or the depths of your depravity by your natural eyes in this age. Only Jesus can see the end from the beginning, and He knows who you will be millions of years from now. He knows where this is going. In the age to come we will see the full truth about all the glory Jesus has given us. It is glory we possess now in His eyes, but we cannot see.

The billionaire and the pauper are the same. They are evaluated by the same set of eyes and the same standard of Jesus. Eternity will tell the truth about who we are, and one day what is real about us will be seen. Right now you are in the "womb of eternity," and you are being fashioned for a day that is yet to come. The pressure, the pain, the pleasure, and the blessings are all part of the Creator's plan to form and fashion you into the image of love equally yoked to Himself in wholehearted abandonment in love. But it must be love defined by Jesus, not by humanism. He is looking for love on His terms. What is that definition? What pleases Him? Our life is found in answering this one question.

4

LIVING FOR LOVE?

THE MEANING OF life is found in the eyes of the One who initiated our lives, and only He has the standard to measure us by. What pleases Jesus? The answer to this question shapes our primary motivation. He not only told us what He was looking for, but He also demonstrated it by the way He lived and died. His entire life is an answer to the search for meaning. By examining His life, we discover the anchor for our existence, purpose, and destiny. We then make it our life aim to find what is pleasing to Jesus, live accordingly, and bring others into that same locked gaze, persuading all men to set their hearts to please Him.

It is not a secret what Jesus is looking for. From the beginning of Genesis to the end of Revelation, over and over again, He has made His desires known. Anyone who wants to please Him can. We can know what pleases Him.

Take the Scripture, "the transcript of His soul," and eat it, feast upon it, and live by every word.

In my search for meaning and purpose I began to devour the words of Jesus and longed to imitate Him in His lifestyle, to walk out every word He had spoken. He not only showed us how to be human by demonstrating perfect humanity, but He also taught us how our own heart fully comes alive. The Scripture is like an instruction manual for humanity. The more I read, the more I began to get caught up in something bigger and Someone greater than me. I am not saying I was caught up in ecstatic experience or euphoria, not at all. Little by little as my view of God changed, my view of the world changed, and inevitably my view of myself changed. As I began to know and understand Jesus, making Him my primary life occupation, my entire life was turned upside down.

LOVE?

I was on this treasure hunt for meaning, and I was discovering the personality of Jesus. I became gripped with His words that summed up all I had previously read and known. He taught that all the law and prophets are summed up in love (Matt. 22:37–40; Rom. 13:8–9). There it is! He summed up the entire purpose of Creation in love. When I first started to see that not only the golden thread woven through Scripture is love but also that love is the lens from which all of life is seen, I was thrown off. I would read through the Gospels, writing down everything that He told me "to do," and then commit to do it. I wanted to be a doer and not just a feeler. Life to me was pragmatic as well as romantic. How could all of life come down to love? It seemed so emotional and not very practical.

Let me stop here and say what love is not. As I am writing, I wish I had another word other than love. In our society *love* is often a cheap word that typically means a strong like or fondness of someone or something. We use the word *love* to describe our most intimate relationships as well as to describe our favorite hamburger place. To some the word *love* means passivity or an acceptance of sin. Others think love is the absence of absolutes in the name of tolerance. To some it is even a representation of their lust.

The kind of love I am talking about has nothing to do with these things. I am talking about the burning desire that pulsated in the heart of the uncreated, causing Him to create an earth filled with a garden and then create mankind out of the dust of that garden and put mankind right next to Him with affection and desire. I am talking about God's story and the dream of His heart. We cannot jump into the meaning of life without getting into His story. When I talk of love, I am talking of holy, transcendent love that is the fountain of all desire and the source of all that exists because it is God Himself. When Jesus said that all of the law and prophets are summed up in love, He is saying that they all define love and facilitate love for Him. It all hangs on love.

THE WHY BEHIND THE WHAT

> "Teacher, which is the great commandment in the law?" Jesus said to him, "'You shall love the LORD your God with all your heart, with all your soul, and with all your mind.' This is the first and great commandment. And the second is like it: 'You shall love your neighbor as yourself.'"
>
> —MATTHEW 22:36–39

This commandment reflects God's ultimate purpose for Creation, His eternal purpose. Here He is standing in front of them, the Creator, and He is answering the question that was meant to trick Him. He knows their hearts and gives them the most profound answer. He wraps all of the law and the prophets into one glorious answer. So much is in these simple few sentences. It would take a thousand books to unpack it and an eternity to unleash the truths that are layered here. From before the foundation of the world God had a plan in His heart. Before the world was created He had a why behind the what. We know what happened: He created the heavens and the earth. But this commandment tells us why He created. We know what He did on the cross: He accomplished redemption. But this verse tells us why He went to the cross. It gives us the why behind the what of Creation and redemption.

The Father promised His Son an inheritance. That inheritance is a people whom He would totally possess. But Jesus's inheritance involves more than real estate. It is more than the reality that He owns the land in every nation. It is more than government. It is more than the fact that He controls the nations and leads them. Jesus's inheritance does involve the mandatory obedience of all of creation, but there is more to His inheritance than only this.

In Philippians 2 Paul gives us insight into this global obedience. He is quoting Isaiah 45:23 where the Father promised the Son in the Old Testament that "every knee should bow...every tongue should confess" (Phil. 2:10–11). Every knee, every tongue, and every demon in hell will bow their knee in obedience. Every unbeliever, when assigned to eternal judgment, will go there in obedience to the word of Jesus. The obedience of all of creation is mandatory. But there is more.

God wants more than mandatory obedience. He wants voluntary love. The inheritance of a king is the obedience of all the nations, but the inheritance of a bridegroom is the voluntary love of all the people in all the nations. The very core of the Bridegroom's inheritance is the fact that the people would be equally yoked to Him in love. The Father promises an inheritance for Jesus, and it is clear that it will be a bride, prepared in love for Him (Rev. 19:7). She will be equally yoked in love—not automated, forced, or programmed, but voluntary love. He said to the Son,

"They will choose You and want You in the same way You choose them and want them." This is the purpose of Creation, the Father preparing an eternal companion for the Son and the Son preparing a family for the Father. The Father prepares us as a bride for His Son, and then, after Jesus brings all the nations under His authority at the end of the millennium, He gives everything to the Father. (See 1 Corinthians 15:27–28.) *We* are the gift they exchange. This blows my mind!

HE IS AFTER MY HEART

In Matthew 22:36–39 Jesus is giving us His own commentary on Deuteronomy 6:5. Of course He is the One who gave it to Moses, but He is adding something that Moses did not receive. He said, "This is the first and great commandment" (Matt. 22:38). This commentary from Jesus has been greatly overlooked and dismissed throughout history. Jesus the great teacher, the great prophet, the great philosopher, the great psychologist, and God Himself is explaining both God and humans to those who have ears to hear. It is the Creator talking, and He is not commanding us to do something that is beyond what we were designed to do. It is love that He is after. He is after our heart. The mystery of our life is found in this truth.

Jesus is saying that loving Him is the first commandment. It is first in priority to Him and to His Father. It is the preeminent command and the pinnacle of all that He has spoken. It is also the greatest commandment, because it has the greatest impact on us, on Him, and literally on the earth. When we love Him with this kind of wholeness, we are what we were created to be. It is just, right, and good. This is righteousness in action. We fulfill our primary purpose in this love. It is the great commandment, and it is the greatest calling.

Some who seek to know God's will for their life focus on knowing what they are supposed to do instead of who they are supposed to become. When they speak of wanting the greatest calling, they refer to the size of their ministry instead of the size of their heart. The greatest grace we can receive is the anointing to feel God's love and to express it. It brings the greatest freedom and has the greatest reward.

I read this and thought, "What? The first and the greatest?" It was perplexing because on the surface it seemed too simple to be the first and the greatest. Yet as I started trying to do it, I found it was the trigger that caused a chain reaction in my heart that led to many life-altering decisions, both internally and externally. These sentences from the lips of Jesus started a fire in my soul and radically changed the course of my life. My purpose in life was to please Jesus, and here He is telling me what pleases Him. So my purpose was to live for love, but what was love?

I drank from the words of Jesus and struggled with their application. When I decided to "live for love," I liked the feeling of it but didn't know what it meant. "Love? OK…and then what?" I looked up at Him and said, "OK, let's do it. I'm going to love You with all of my heart, soul, mind, and strength…OK, now what? I love You. You love Me." I sang a few songs, danced, and cried during the Sunday morning worship time. "OK…" I lit a candle and sat in a room for a while talking to the Invisible. "I love You. You love me. Is this what You wanted? Is this what You were saying was the pinnacle and purpose of my life? Surely there's more to it than this."

Then I started trying to love Him with "all." It was more than an emotion because of a good worship song and more than an hour of devotional time in the morning. I read this verse and thought, "He wants all of me." He wanted to be involved in every part of my day, right down to the thoughts I think and the emotions I feel. I was overwhelmed with such a demand but excited to have an aim. It was more than a list of dos and don'ts. This was up close and personal. This was intimate and invasive.

Three of the four ways He lists for us to love Him are primarily internal. Only He can see it working. This command had nothing to do with impressing people or getting the applause of man. This commandment brought me right before the Audience of One and turned my primary mode of living internal, because that is where He was and that is where He was watching and measuring me.

The inner world of the human is one of the most

intriguing realities in all of creation. We spend the majority of our lives inside of ourselves. We are sleeping, thinking quietly, processing images, and having a continual conversation in our heads. I could be in a stadium filled with eighty thousand people, and we are all thinking eighty thousand different things, having eighty thousand conversations in our own heads, living in a world of our own, like a universe of worlds inhabiting a larger one. The internal world is vast and limitless. It is where the Spirit lives and it is where Jesus's eyes of fire are looking (Rev. 2:18). He measures us by what we do in our follow-through, as well as by what we do in our hearts. It is both internal and external, but I fear most of us neglect the inside, and the inside is what shapes the outside. I will develop this further in the coming chapters.

THE MIND

Have you ever tried to love God with all of your mind? The mind is so sacred, yet we severely and criminally waste it. The human mind is of great value, and it is at the mercy of the free will of the man or woman who possesses it. What we choose to put in our minds shapes our hearts and our emotions, and this shapes our decisions and our entire life experience. The mind is one of the crucial, defining things about humans. I am not just talking about the intellect, in the sense of our IQ, but the things we behold with our minds, we become. This means that the things we fill our minds with, we become like.

It is incomprehensible to me the amount of time we spend watching TV, movies, searching the web, watching YouTube videos, and just marinating our brains in sitcom humor and raw stupidity in the name of "rest" or "entertainment." We do not understand that hours and hours of this plants seeds into the soil of our minds that are not immediately reaped, but over time the fruit of this kind of waste will be seen as our minds grow dull, causing our spirits to grow dull. (See Galatians 6:8.) A dullness in spirit causes our connection with the Lord to grow dull, leading to despair and meaninglessness, which leads to sin.

It all starts in the mind. The amount of time spent on meaningless things is so devastating. I believe when we get to heaven, one of our primary regrets will be the amount of worthless things we gave our minds to. One day all will be clear, and we will see the gift that God gave us in giving the sacred space of the mind. We will take a few steps back and see how we squandered it and the potential we had to encounter God that we did not take, and we will feel regret.

I don't want to have regret on that day. I don't want to have regret tonight as I go to bed and close my eyes, only to see the video games I played the previous four hours before the light went out, or worse, the immorality I was watching or the coarse jesting I was hearing. You cannot get these things out of your mind once you put them in, and yet we just walk through the wet cement of our minds leaving a mess that will dry and take the mercy of God and a shocking sledgehammer to break up and renew. I want to feel the dignity that has been given to me, that I am not at the mercy of vain imagination and worthless things.

It is not easy. I am prone to laziness and ease. I want to "check out" and just "hang out" for a while. I cannot tell you how many young people who started out fiery for God who I have seen lose their way in pursuing God with wholeheartedness, because they lost the reins of their minds through entertainment or hours spent in vain debate. It is hard to get someone who chooses to go down this path to turn around because they lose their vision for depth in God and lose their vision for purpose. It is hard to get them out of their aimless state. I have fear about this because of my own propensity to idleness and to foolishness. Loving God with all of your mind is not a small thing. In your mind is a perpetual conversation you cannot turn off. It is a perpetual movie screen that you cannot escape. You cannot go to "nothing" and empty your mind. You cannot turn it off, even when you sleep.

It is the theater where God wants to be seen by you, but very few people will ever look at Him here. I have such compulsive, addictive tendencies that I will literally spend hours in Google searches only to realize I have wasted that sacred space of my mind. I will get lost in the social networking world, where I am in a constant conversation with other people. Some people are texting all day long.

If you are in a perpetual conversation with other people,

that conversation is getting in the space where you were created to talk to God. It is like the Lord cannot get a word in edgewise, and then we look up and accuse Him of silence. Yet we don't stop talking long enough to listen to Him, and we don't actually talk to Him. Even in our quiet times when we are alone, we are tweeting, texting, Facebooking, e-mailing, and searching the Internet. Obviously some of this is good, but if you are like me and have a tendency to be compulsive or addictive, beware, because days will go by, and they will turn into weeks and then months and years, and you will rarely talk to God or even think about Him in a direct way. That most holy place of your mind will be full of junk piles that will take great effort to clean out.

I have the fear of the Lord concerning being held accountable for my mind. All too often we think that we are at the mercy of our imagination or at the mercy of our thoughts, but we must learn to take the reins of our mind, renew it with the Word, and be transformed because of it.

> Do not be conformed to this world, but be transformed by the renewing of your mind, that you may prove what is that…perfect will of God.
> —ROMANS 12:2

The mind is the seedbed for life. Both righteousness and wickedness start in the mind. Jesus said adultery starts in the mind. All manner of sin starts here, and so does righteousness. We set our mind on things above (Col. 3:2), and we become what we behold in our minds (2 Cor. 3:18). This means that what we look at, what we mediate on, and what we fill the sacred space of our mind with we become. This is a scary idea and one that most do not take very seriously. It is also a powerful idea when applied to righteousness.

How to Love Jesus With Your Mind

First, you must see that He loves you with all of His mind. What He is asking from you is not what He Himself doesn't already do (1 John 4:19). Imagine, how vast is God's mind? Look at the universe and all of its intricacies; from the galaxies to the dandelion, creation is stunning. Yet He loves us with His mind.

Secondly, you must believe that He sees your mind, and what goes on in your head matters to Him. He is looking at the thoughts and intentions of man, not just their actions. He actually has capacity to see your mind. No human can do this. I cannot see what is going on, on the other side of your face, even when I am sitting directly in front of you. I do not know what you are thinking until you tell me, but Jesus sees it all (Heb. 4:13).

Thirdly, you have to believe that it is not only possible to love Him with all of your mind, but also that you will be most happy and fully alive as you pursue this.

Fourthly, you must not give up. You will not love Him with "all" the moment you set your intentions to do it. It is a lifelong journey He wants you to go on. Trust me, this loving Him with all of your mind will cause you to make many life decisions that will alter the course of your life. It is stunning to me how well He knows us. He knew if He started in the center of man, it would affect the whole man and all that is around that man. Jesus starts in the center, confidently knowing it will shape the entire man into an image of love He could have never attained if He started on the outside. Again we are transformed by the renewing of our minds (Rom. 12:2).

Loving God with your mind includes what you believe about God, His personality, His essence, everything about Him. It includes the pursuit of truth and ideas. It is what you come into agreement with concerning the truth about God, yourself, life, your worldview, your philosophy, and your theology. The mind is the intellect, but it is not only the intellectual, it is also theatrical. It is a movie screen with continual images and a perpetual conversation.

The mind is designed for meditation. It is the doorway to the spirit of man, where God dwells. God gave you an imagination, and the goal is not to overcome it but use it. You will never overcome it, because it is part of your human design, and He created you with the capacity to visualize the Scripture. I will talk more about this in the coming chapters.

I want to love Him with all of my mind, where He becomes my favorite thought. I want Him to be the place I naturally go when I am driving in my car or when I am quietly "just thinking." I want Him to become my daydream, my natural thought, my first thought and my last. I want Him to be my resting place, and I want to be His. In all honesty, thinking about God is often an effort. He is not a natural thought. I say, "Lord, help me to love You with all of my mind." The mind has to be renewed, and it is a seedbed where what we sow, we reap; but it is a continual sowing and reaping. He will help us, though, if we ask. He will help us, and He sees the reaching even before we attain the fullness.

HEART

The mind is where it starts, and the heart is like the undercurrent. Now let me say, it is difficult to try and perfectly distinguish between the mind, heart, and soul. In the Scripture sometimes these terms are used for the same thing with subtle distinctions. I don't want to spend too much time trying to define each of them and their differences, but with broad strokes I will continue.

We are to engage our emotions in our love for God. God wants more than dutiful service. Our love for God touches our emotions without succumbing to emotionalism. We have a significant role in determining how our emotions develop over time. We can cultivate greater affections for God by setting our hearts to grow in this sphere. We can "set" our love or affections on anything we choose. Our emotions eventually follow whatever we set ourselves to pursue. This involves determining that the primary dream of our hearts is to walk in the first commandment.

As we change our minds, the Spirit changes our hearts and our emotions. We set our hearts first on loving Jesus and causing others to love Him. "Because he has set his love [heart] upon Me, therefore I will deliver him" (Ps. 91:14). David made a choice to set his heart to love God. He determined to love God: "I will love You, O LORD, my strength" (Ps. 18:1).

Our emotions are a very important and powerful part of our life. Thus, God wants to be loved from this part of our life. The heart must be kept focused and clean with diligence. We keep our hearts by refusing to allow our emotions to be inappropriately connected to money, positions of honor, wrong relationships, sinful addictions, bitterness, offenses, and so on. Proverbs 4:23 says, "Keep your heart with all diligence, for out of it spring the issues of life."

Christianity is an ongoing encounter of love with a Person. Possessing fierce dedication will not keep us steady unless we encounter love at the heart level. We resist being entrenched in vain imaginations that cause our emotions to be progressively stirred by various lusts. We express our love to God by resisting emotions contrary to His will. To love Him with all of our hearts is to have undivided affection, giving Him exclusive possession of our hearts. It is from the heart of man that passion rises, and it is the passion of man that drives him. We want to be obsessed with Jesus, preoccupied with passionate pursuit of Him. This takes a supernatural working of the Holy Spirit. We cannot do this on our own, but we can set our hearts on the journey.

I want to actually feel affection for Jesus when I close my eyes and talk to Him. Even the desire to love Him is evidence of love, not the absence. Our desire for Him is a supernatural gift, and even though our hearts often feel dull or preoccupied with other loves, if we set our love on Him and set Him on our hearts, over time our hearts will be filled with the fire of love. It takes time, though, and it is a battle. If it were automatic, it would not be love. The continual choices we make to daily pull our hearts away from other loves and untangle our affections is love itself. The actual choices, even though they are sometimes painful, are an expression of love and will position us to feel the fire of God over time. Our hearts will actually change.

SOUL

The soul is your personality. It is what makes you, you. The soul is what makes people different. It's the angle from which you see life. It is your identity and your unique personality. We realign our identity to be based on our relationship with God instead of on our accomplishments and the recognition we receive from people. Our identity is determined by the way we define our success and value, thus, by how we see ourselves. When we get our identity from our accomplishments and recognition, we end up in an emotional storm of preoccupation with vanity. We most naturally see our accomplishments as very small and unimportant, causing us to feel rejected and neglected by people.

We must define our primary success in life as being ones who are loved by Jesus and who love Him in return. This is what determines our personal worth. We are to be anchored in this truth as the basis of our success and worth rather than in our accomplishments, recognition, or possessions. Our identity must be established on being loved by God and in loving Him in response. Our confession is, "I am loved by God, and I am a lover of God; therefore I am successful."

We will love Jesus much better with less "emotional traffic" inside our soul. We have to regularly refocus our soul and anchor our identity in our ultimate purpose, letting the secondary things take second place so that we are not tossed on the sea of vanity.

STRENGTH

Our strength is expressed through the way we use our resources. We are to love God with our strength, which means instead of our usual way of using our resources to increase our personal comfort and honor. We should also use them to invest directly in building the kingdom. God cares about the love we show Him when we invest our strength into our relationship with Him and in helping others to love Him. We show our strength in five activities, as seen in the center section of the Sermon on the Mount.

1. Blessing our adversaries (Matt. 5:43–48; 6:14–15)

2. Serving (Matt. 6:1–4)

3. Praying (Matt. 6:5–13)

4. Fasting from food (Matt. 6:16–18)

5. Giving (Matt. 6:19–21)

God multiplies and then returns our strengths back to us. However, He does it in His own timing and way. This takes faith that God is watching and that He esteems this as an expression of love. I will develop this more in the next chapter.

Loving God with our strength involves our money, time, physical strength, and abilities. He wants us to love Him in this way, not because He needs our money or contribution, but because when we offer it to Him in love, there are many human dynamics that happen. When we transfer our confidence from our money to God, by giving extravagantly, we are loving Him. When we transfer our rights to use our time the way we want by spending time in prayer and in serving others to show Him love, He sees it.

When we obey the Lord in these arenas of our strength, we press to love Him by giving above and beyond what most would think to give. This is so important to understand because some just think of loving God in a worship service and in a general way of emotion, but we want to love Him with our strength. Our love is tangible and has action in it. We know that even though we are weak, this will take us into a deeper level of love.

I have sought to love Him, and I have found the pressure points in money, time, words, and physical strength. When I surrender these to Him, I feel the pain in my flesh (or natural self) and say, "Ouch, Lord. I didn't know about that fear I had in money. I guess I didn't trust You as much as I thought. I want to love You here." Or, "That was humiliating to not defend myself when I had smart answers to give," yet I choose to love Him by giving up the strength of my words. I fast and feel the physical weakness but find His strength. He says, "Love Me with all of your strength by fasting in these arenas." That is what is meant by loving Him with all your strength. I will develop this further in the next chapter.

ALL

The reason Jesus asks us to love Him with all of our heart, soul, mind, and strength is because that is how He loves us. Paul wrote that God's love is beyond our ability to fully comprehend without the Holy Spirit's help and the time span of eternity to discover more and more of it (Eph. 3:18–19). We cannot comprehend the vast ocean of God's love, but when we see His high demand for "all," we see He is not asking anything from us He Himself does not give. We are equally yoked to Jesus not by the size of our love but by the all of our love. Though our all is small, is it still our all. The Lord values our commitment to continually grow in love. The reach of our heart to love Him moves Him. If we do not quit, then we win.

We come to the place where we no longer find our identity in our failure but in the fact that God loves us, in the gift of righteousness (2 Cor. 5:17), and in the cry of our spirit to love God. Our weak attempts move Him, and this is when life becomes meaningful and dynamic. The purpose of life is to love Him with our all and to be loved by Him. As we are seeing, this is no small task, but it is a life-consuming journey that affects everything about us. We have been given this dignity called the free will. This free will enables us to choose, and when we choose to give Jesus what He wants, it moves Him deeply. The fact that we can move God gives our lives more meaning and more purpose than anything.

THE SECOND IS LIKE IT

The second commandment cannot be separated from the first. Jesus Himself said that you cannot say you love Him and hate your brother. Love is a progression:

1. We have to see that Jesus loves us. The Holy Spirit reveals this to us. We only love because we are first loved (1 John 4:19). We cannot love Him until we first see that He loves us. This is why the primary way

that we grow in affection for Him is by meditating on His affections for us.

2. We love Jesus in response to His great love for us.

3. We love ourselves. Whenever we see ourselves caught up in the bigger story of Jesus and we see His great love for us, we begin to love Him in return, and our view of ourselves changes. We no longer live in self-hatred, wishing we were someone else or had been given a better lot in life. The reason many do not love their neighbor is because they do not love themselves, and they have envy or annoyance for others. You will never love your neighbor in greater quality than you love yourself in the grace of God.

4. We love others.

This is all supernatural. It takes the operation of the gift of the Holy Spirit. The greatest gift and work of the Holy Spirit in a believer's life is to pour love into the heart in these four ways. You cannot come into contact with the fire of love and not love others. It is impossible. Jesus loves humans so much He died for them. He is the great evangelist and greatly desires humanity. When we come into contact with Him, we will love others. We will also be formed into His image, and as bearers of His name we will love others as He loves them.

There is a lifestyle of love that enables us to love Him and to love others, but at first glance it seems upside down and backward. Jesus made the way to please Him so simple that anyone can do it, yet few will. It is not too mysterious or far away. He has not been silent as to how He measures us. The challenge is walking it out and staying steady for decades.

5

THE INSIDE-OUT, UPSIDE-DOWN KINGDOM

JESUS DEFINED LOVING Him as being deeply rooted in a spirit of obedience. There is no such thing as loving God without seeking to obey Him—not because He is a tyrant, but because He knows us best and He knows the best way to bring us forth in love. His commandments are the pathway to love and life. He said, "If you love Me, keep My commandments....He who has My commandments and keeps them, it is he who loves Me....If anyone loves Me, he will keep my word" (John 14:15–23).

"If anyone loves Me, he will keep My word." What could be confusing about that statement? Three times, within several verses, Jesus makes it clear how He defines loving Him. From Genesis to Revelation He makes it clear. Yet it is strange how nebulous and how blurred many are on this definition. There is no such thing as loving Jesus without seeking to obey His words. It is a deception. It is a religious figment of someone's imagination and nothing more than religious sentiment. The Holy Spirit will not bare witness to it on the last day, and Jesus will not buy it at the judgment seat. God requires more than singing to Him about love or writing poems about love. He requires more than sentimental feelings.

There is an unholy momentum in the nations where more and more people, who, in the name of Jesus, are making Him into the image of what they want in a god. Then they are defining love according to the god that they created. It is not Jesus.

One of the core issues of conflict of the generation in which the Lord returns will be the definition of love. Do we love on God's terms, or do we love on the terms of the humanistic culture that has no reference to obedience to what He has already spoken? We must love Jesus with the intention to "keep His commandments" because Scripture is our pathway to Him and the standard that we will be evaluated by. We can't say that we love Him and then refuse the path that leads to Him. That would be like saying you love someone in a foreign country but you refuse to look at them, talk to them on the phone, read their messages, get on an airplane to see them, or even speak the same language as them. This isn't love.

Jesus's commandments are the tracks that lead to Him. If you love Him, you will take the train and find Him.

That does not mean our obedience is mature or that we never fail. I often fail and come up short in my obedience, but my heart is set to obey the written Word of God, most specifically the Sermon on the Mount (Matt. 5–7). It is the clearest definition of love in the Bible. There it is in three chapters.

HE OWNS US

Jesus doesn't only want to forgive us; He also wants to own us. He wants to brand us with His name, to mark us and claim us as His own possession. He wants us to bear His name so that everything that is His is ours. It is the meek who will inherit it (Matt. 5:5). Your freedom is in the yoke of Christ and in binding yourself to Him and throwing away the key. I want to be a prisoner of love, bound by affection, motivated by desire, and clinging to Jesus by giving Him control of my life.

Right at the beginning of the Sermon on the Mount He makes it clear that He wants the whole of you, not just your deeds but also your heart. It involves more than a checklist; it involves every part of your being, right down to your thoughts. He wants to fully possess you and transform you into the image of love. We transfer the rights of our life into His hands by obeying His written Word. When you agreed to accept His blood for the forgiveness of your sins, you were entering into a covenant to give yourself to Jesus. You do not own yourself any longer. You belong to a Master, and your freedom is found in His words.

It is the most liberating way to live, to live in love. You were created for it. The good thing about His commandments is His heart behind them. All of His commandments lead us to Him, and they lead us to freedom. That's the stunning part. Many people are wrapped in the heavy chains of darkness, with the master called Sin standing above them, with a whip of fear, shame, regret, anger, depression, lust, and pride, but they are refusing the yoke of Christ in the name of "freedom." This is irrational. You will be bound, one way or the other, either by sin and darkness or by Love Himself.

I gladly yoke myself to Jesus, even though it is not always easy and I fail many times. His commandments are a delight to my soul and a lamp to my feet. We want to run the course of His commands, knowing that they create in us His original intention and design and therefore our ultimate purpose.

DISCIPLED BY JESUS

There is coming a day when each one of us will stand before the Man with fiery eyes, the same Jesus that John the Beloved saw in the Book of Revelation (Rev. 1:12–17). He is the Man who has fire in His eyes, and only His evaluation will stand. He has not been silent on what His standard is. He both demonstrated it and taught it when He was walking on this earth. Then He sent us His Spirit to help us in our weakness. He enjoys the process of our transformation. We can all have gold in the day we stand before Him if we want it, but it will cost everything. (See 1 Corinthians 3:11–15.)

The true measure of a man can be measured only according to Jesus's lifestyle and words. Our definition of success can be defined only by Jesus's words and by looking at His life on the earth and imitating Him. This is the only definition of success that will carry over to the age to come, and this is the only path to eternal purpose and eternal greatness.

Love is demonstrated through lives that imitate Love Himself. Jesus showed us what love is when He walked on the earth. The lifestyle He lived was meant to be seen as the greatest expression of love. Those who want to love Him will imitate Him and be disciples of His words. We want to be disciples of Jesus, not of men, because only Jesus has the standard to measure us by and only He knows what an ideal human should be. We must love Him on His terms. The good news is it is so simple anyone can do it. The bad news is it is so simple few will. It is simple but costly.

It costs everything to love Jesus the way He loves us because He gave everything. This is why He asks us to do the same. The Sermon on the Mount defines love on God's terms. He is not asking us to do anything He did not do. He ran the race ahead of us to show us the way it is to be done (Heb. 6:20). He showed us what it means to be human. Jesus lived before the eyes of His Father, committing His ways and His destiny to His Father. Even when His life looked in vain and as though He had spent His strength for nothing (Isa. 49:4), He cast Himself into the hands of the Father and lived before His eyes without defending Himself or making sure He "got what He deserved." So much of the Sermon on the Mount is about transferring our confidence in making our lives matter from our own hands into the hands of the Father.

Jesus is meek in His heart. This is not passivity; this is "power in restraint." He is the God of all creation who walked the streets of Jerusalem, hid His glory, and even died at the hands of the people He created in order to show the lengths love would go. How can the Genesis 1 God be so passionately humble? It is His glory that causes Him to be like this. The yoke of meekness is the yoke that He wears. He wants to bind us to Himself in it, because it is how He is at the heart level (Matt. 11:28–30). The Sermon on the Mount is the way into the yoke of Jesus. It is the "easy yoke" once you get it on but putting it on requires "spiritual violence" (v. 12). This is the true measure of a man, and it seems inside out and upside down.

I love the way Jesus set up His kingdom. It is upside down right now, and things look backward. He has made it so simple. To go high, you just go low. To become rich, you become poor. Anyone can go low and poor. Anyone, everyone, can serve and walk in humility. I adore Jesus, because He says that "they [the meek] shall inherit the earth" (Matt. 5:5), and "the first will be last, and the last will be first" (Mark 10:31). No one can accuse Him of being unfair or unjust, because anyone can do this and therefore fulfill his primary life purpose by being pleasing in His sight. Literally anyone can do it, except the proud. I think that we will be shocked at some of the men and women He "crowns and robes" in that day, because they were men and women we overlooked or shunned in this age. We cannot measure one another, because we cannot see what He sees. He knows the heart of man, and He sees in secret (Matt. 6:1–6, 18).

SPIRITUAL MOURNING

The Sermon on the Mount is the way to walk out the first and second commandment. Yet the more I tried to live it, the more I seemed to fail. The more I tried to love God with all of my heart, soul, mind, and strength and to love others, the more aware I was of my need for Him. It is impossible to love God without supernatural help. I looked at the Sermon on the Mount as an expression of love for Jesus and for mankind, and I saw how short I was falling. I would cry out for help and weep in my immaturity, and then, to my surprise, this whole exercise ended up producing the very attitudes Jesus called blessed!

I will never forget the day I was crying in failure, feeling as though I would never love Jesus and that I was doomed to a life of continually coming up short. My heart was breaking because of how easily I strayed from truth and how quickly I turned from the Lord. I was weeping because I genuinely wanted to love Him but could not seem to get there. As I cried, a friend looked at me and said, "Blessed are those who mourn, for they shall be comforted. Blessed are those who hunger for righteousness, for they shall be filled." He went on to say that the emotion I was feeling was the evidence of love, not the absence of it. He said that my mourning for righteousness was proof that the seeds were growing in the soil of my soul and that I would, in time, reap the fruit of it if I persevered. This is stunning.

Right at the beginning of Jesus's sermon He is saying that longing to love Him and to walk in righteousness is a blessed thing, even before we attain it. Trying to live the Sermon on the Mount and failing created this spiritual mourning, which was what He wanted in the first place. It caused me to lean on Him and not my own strength. When my friend said this to me, it was as though a light went on in my heart, and I began to realize that what Jesus was after in this life was not perfection, as we define it, but humility and perseverance. He values humility and perseverance more than instant perfection. That is why life and love are a process.

THE WAR ON THE INSIDE

I never was a fan of process. Being a very impatient person, I always want to "get to the point." I am the type who wants to get to the punch line, and I am often perturbed by process. Jesus is very different. His kingdom is like a seed that takes time to grow and bear fruit. One of the primary purposes of life is the process and what it produces in us. If everything were instant, what would we do for all of eternity?

Jesus loves the process and is patient with us in our weakness. The Sermon on the Mount starts the process of transformation that happens in the soul and life of the person who loves Him. It has the power to transform you. It's the law of the kingdom that starts internally and seemingly insignificant. This sermon is bizarre in its application, because it goes against the stream of our natural impulses to defend ourselves, be greedy, stay comfortable, and to make sure everyone knows how devout we are. All of these are natural tendencies that we have from birth, and they are curbed by the hand of the Potter when we yield to His glorious words in this simple sermon. At first read it may not seem that powerful, but try to live it 100 percent, and you will feel the heat of transformation as you realize that so much of it is the opposite of your natural bend and the opposite of the lust and pride of life. This is because Jesus is so much different than we are. He is love, and therefore, He is humility.

When I was in my early twenties, I became hooked on the Sermon on the Mount. I would corner anyone who gave me the chance and preach it as the lifestyle of love. As I tried to live it out, something in me started to change. The change was not due to living by a set of rules, like some kind of checklist. But I was being transformed, because so much of this sermon is what is done in secret. Over and over Jesus is saying, "My eyes are on you, and everything you do matters. I call it love every time you choose Me, every time you reach for righteousness, every time you turn the other cheek, go the extra mile, refuse to worry about your life. All of this I see as love, and it moves My heart."

The war on the inside of us is the arena in which we can choose to demonstrate love. That same choice Adam was given in the garden is the same choice we are given time after time. When we choose righteousness, humility, love, and meekness, we are demonstrating not only our allegiance to Jesus but also our affection for Him.

The more I allowed the Sermon on the Mount to be my guide, the more determined I became to walk it out to the utmost. Servanthood, fasting, prayer, a secret life, love for enemies, all of these things He calls love. My life calling is to live before His eyes by walking out His commandments as the instruction manual for my heart and life, confidently knowing that He is watching and that He calls it love. He sees in secret, and it doesn't matter how many people notice or don't notice; only His evaluation matters at the end of the day. We know how we will be measured. He has made it clear that the standard we will be measured with on the day we meet Him face-to-face is the standard of Scripture. The Sermon on the

Mount is one of the primary places that He has made that standard clear.

I will give you a couple of examples of the transforming power of this sermon. Jesus said, "Whoever slaps you on your right check, turn the other to him also" (Matt. 5:39). This is not talking about being physically assaulted. It is talking about being insulted. For a man to slap another man on the face was an insult. Jesus is saying, "Do not to defend yourself when you are insulted." There are many times I want to defend myself or prove myself when I feel misunderstood. I can hear the whisper of Jesus, telling me that my reputation is in His hands, not mine. This is a hard one for most people because we naturally want to defend and define ourselves, but He is our defender, and He is the one who defines us. Keeping silent before misunderstanding has always been a challenge and one that I have not always done well, but He sees this struggle and calls it love. Making this choice time after time changes me.

Here's another example of the transforming power of His words: Jesus exposed how the spirit of immorality operates by telling us that it is rooted first in the mind. Again, He wants the whole person. He said, "Whoever looks at a woman to lust...has already committed adultery...in his heart" (v. 28). The progression of adultery is lust of the eye leads to adultery in the heart, which leads to circumstances, and then on to physical adultery. The principle is immorality is established first in the area of the eyes. Jesus wants us to understand the role of the "eye gate" as the primary battlefront for stopping the operation of the sin. This applies to all manner of sin, not only sexual sin. It is easier to close the "eye gate" than to put out the fires of immoral passions.

When I read this, I realize Jesus isn't only asking me to restrain my actions but also to start at the root. He deals with the very root of lust and teaches us how to be transformed at the heart level. This causes me to recognize sin before it has blossomed, and this transforms me from the inside out.

This is where the battle begins. God is often seen pleading with His people, because their hearts were far away from Him. He is after our hearts, and He wants us entirely. There is a war on the inside, and it is the theater where we can demonstrate love. We make choices to live in meekness and servanthood as demonstrated by Jesus and taught in the Sermon on the Mount. It is more than just the setting of my mind and my affections. I have the arena of life to demonstrate love. Every time I choose righteousness and humility, He calls it love. I now had something to "do" to demonstrate love.

A tool that has helped me to grasp this sermon is an outline by Mike Bickle. He says:

> The Sermon on the Mount (Matt. 5-7) defines love on God's terms. It calls us to live out the eight Beatitudes (Matt. 5:3–12) as we pursue

hundredfold obedience (Matt. 5:48) by resisting the six negative influences related to our natural lusts (Matt. 5:21–48) and by pursuing the five positive nutrients (Matt. 6:10–18) that position us to receive the Spirit's impartation of grace. We measure our ministry impact by the extent to which those we minister to live out these values, not by the number of people who receive our ministry.[1]

There are many books written on this great sermon, and I will not take time to break it all down for you here. I encourage you to make it one of your life aims to search it out and to live it. Here are some commentaries that I recommend on the Sermon on the Mount:

- *Studies in the Sermon on the Mount* by D. Martyn Lloyd-Jones

- *The Message of the Sermon on the Mount* by John R. W. Stott

- *The Sermon on the Mount* by R. T. Kendall

- *Jesus' Sermon on the Mount and His Confrontation With the World* by D. A. Carson

There are many more you will find if you make this a treasure you seek.

If you try and live this 100 percent and combine it with seeing how He feels about you in your immaturity, you will be transformed. You will not be transformed instantly. Remember, life and love are a process, and Jesus likes the process. You will fail many times, but even the failing produces the heart attitudes He wants if you are sincerely reaching for 100 percent obedience. Stay with it, keep reaching, and don't give up. If you don't quit, you'll win.

Do not measure your growth in one or two years, but over decades you will see how you have changed. Don't get caught up in how far you have come or the ground that you have lost. Just keep your eyes ahead and let Him measure you in the last day; don't measure yourself. You must see how He feels about you in the process in order to sustain the reach. When we first start to try and love Him with all of our heart, soul, mind, and strength, and when we first set our hearts to live the gospel generously, even before we have attained what we set our hearts on, it moves Him deeply. (See Song of Solomon 4:9.)

FREEDOM OF HOLINESS

The clearer picture I had of the answer to what He was looking for and the more confident I became that He liked me while I was in the process of maturing, the more I found freedom in reaching to live wholeheartedly. I found the demands of Jesus were bringing liberation to me because I was becoming unmovable. You cannot touch a person who lives this way. Most of what binds us in this life are things that cause anxiety or darkness, and most of our anxiety is addressed by acting in the opposite spirit, according to the Sermon on the Mount.

Jesus gives us a clear path to freedom from anxiety and sin. It is the freedom of holiness. When you live like this, you have a purpose that transcends pleasing man or even pleasing your own pride and lust, and you become untouchable. I am not saying that you are not affected by the opinion of man or by sin, but you overcome them little by little, and your primary life dream is untouchable. My goal became humility, my road map became the words that Jesus spoke, and every circumstance became an arena to demonstrate love. Even loving my enemies, who at that time were reduced to people who simply annoyed me, became a platform to love Jesus. I wanted to go out of my way to go the extra mile, because I knew He was watching, and He called it love. I wanted to wage war on the desire for comfort, ease, and lesser pleasure, because I wanted to feel more of His superior pleasure. My life began to come alive before His eyes, and there was no one who could touch this vision. It is the unbreakable dream.

It is the upside-down kingdom, and those who live it often look like fools or weak in the eyes of man, but this kind of wisdom will be justified. There are many shining examples throughout history of men and women who have lived this message to extremes, and their lives scream transcendence and point to someone greater. Their very lives are prophetic oracles that declare life is more than meets the eye and there is someone watching who will measure us in the end. I want to have a life that prophesies. I want to actually *be* the message, not just preach it. What compels a person to live this way when it all seems so upside down? Everyone in life is running in the rat race trying to get to the top of the success ladder. We don't want to run the rat race; we want to run the real race—the one that has an eternal prize. That race is found in the words of Jesus. People who live the gospel generously go to extremes in love, and they touch Jesus's heart deeply. The Sermon on the Mount will help to set you on fire, if you live it before the eyes of the One who loves you, with the aid of the Holy Spirit.

"Look at Jesus Only"

When I was a teenager, I read *The Hiding Place* by Corrie ten Boom. I was struck by how often she and her sister Betsie quoted the Sermon on the Mount. You all know the story of Corrie and her family. They were Dutch Christians, living in the Netherlands during World War II. During the Nazi occupation, several members of the ten Boom family got involved with aiding Jews who were in hiding. Corrie, her sister Betsie, and their father, Casper, took in Jews who were trying to escape from the horrors of the Nazis. Eventually Corrie, Betsie, Casper, their brother, Willem, and a nephew were taken to concentration camps where Betsie, their nephew, and Casper died. Willem died after the war from spinal tuberculosis, which he contracted while in prison. Corrie alone survived to tell the story.

The terrors of a concentration camp cannot even be imagined, and their story has pressed my heart to question the purpose of suffering and love. Yet these ladies were burning and shining lamps, unrelenting in devotion to Jesus, eager to please Him. The story that Corrie recalls in her book that is painted on my heart the most is the story of a day when Betsie was carrying rocks, one pile to another. Everyone in the camp was starving and sick. Betsie was especially frail and ill, and she was struggling to keep moving. One of the guards saw her struggling and came over to her and began to give her a hard time and shout out degrading names, demanding that she work harder. The guard then took part of her leather belt and slashed Betsie across the chest and neck. Corrie watched this whole thing feeling helpless and angry. Corrie loved her sister dearly and could do nothing about this injustice and pain being afflicted on her.

Without knowing what she was doing and with murderous anger in her heart, Corrie seized her own shovel and rushed at the guard. Betsie stopped her and said, "Corrie! Corrie, keep working!"

Corrie then saw the welt on Betsie's neck, and Betsie said, "Don't look at it, Corrie. Look at Jesus only."[2]

She appealed to Corrie to look to Jesus, to choose love despite what the guard had just done to her. Right then and there, at the point of severe human suffering, the reality of Betsie's relationship with Jesus made her untouchable. Yes, her body ached. Yes, her heart hurt, but she refused to be brought to the level of evil. She chose to live above it.

In another scene Betsie encouraged others in the Lord:

> Jesus knows every one of your feelings. He prays with you when two or more get together to pray. He promised He would be there, even in Ravensbruck! In our lives before, we were separated by so much, but here, all of that has been stripped away, and we see the truth. Jesus in each one of us. Light in this darkness, and we can praise Him together![3]

Then they begin to pray together. Betsie prayed for her persecutors as Jesus commanded us to do: "Father, bless the German people from Your great storehouse of love. Forgive them, for Jesus' sake. Do not hold this place to their charge. Forgive them, even before they know to ask."[4]

I would have loved to have seen the look on Jesus's face as His heart was so deeply moved by the devotion of this woman. She believed He was watching her, and she believed her heart responses mattered to Him. She believed life was bigger than a momentary suffering, and she had allowed true compassion and true love to be formed in her heart, to the point where she felt genuine love for a real enemy. This is a work of the Holy Spirit and a testimony of transcendence. These are the kind of men and women the world is not worthy of.

There are a multitude of stories throughout history when men and women lived the gospel generously and to the fullest of their capacity. These are the stories I love to feast on and mediate on. These are the people I want to run the race with. I don't want to compare myself with the people in my generation and feel good about how godly I am because I give a little more money or spend a little more time in prayer than my neighbor. I want to run the race with men and women such as John the Baptist and all who have followed him who take the words of Jesus at face value and truly become people the world is not worthy of.

We cannot do this in our own strength. It is impossible to please Jesus and to transform ourselves without divine help. We are in great need, and the longer I press for a life of wholeheartedness, the more I see my need. The older I get, the harder it gets, not easier. I want to run the race with endurance, but I need the aid of someone bigger. It takes the help of God Himself in order to stay in the furnace of transformation. We often start off with a lot of zeal and then run out of steam very quickly. We need the fire of God Himself to energize us, sustain us, and keep us steadfast to the end. We need Him to help us.

FIRE OF LOVE: SUSTAINED BY GOD

A WISE MAN ONCE said, "It takes God to love God." The longer I am on this journey of loving Him, the more I realize what a true statement this is. It is impossible to sustain a genuine love for Jesus and for others without the aid of the Holy Spirit. We do not have the capacity to live the gospel wholeheartedly or to have hearts that are full of affection for Jesus without a supernatural Helper to guide us into that love (Rom. 5:5).

Jesus told us to love Him with all of our heart, soul, mind, and strength (Matt. 22:37), but it is an impossible command unless we combine it with what Jesus taught us in the Gospel of John. He tells us to abide in Him (John 15:4–5). We are in great need and desperately dependent. We never outgrow our constant need to be helped, guided, taught, and counseled by God Himself. This is yet another statement of His great zeal for us as individuals and how He wants us to lean on Him, daily relying on Him. This requires a regular encounter with God.

Many people today talk about encountering God, and I am not sure what they mean by that phrase. Sometimes they are talking about having manifestations, such as shaking or falling over in a prayer line. Others are talking about getting a breakthrough in provision or healing. I believe in these kinds of encounters, but there is something even greater, even more exhilarating, even more sustaining and addicting; it is when God Himself reveals God to our hearts. When we feel love for Him and from Him, if even for a moment, we feel the heat of His heart touch ours. This holy kiss is enough to set us on a ravenous treasure hunt the rest of our lives. We will do anything to just experience that touch once more. In this holy exchange we are touching our primary life purpose, which is to be with God. All humans were created for this divine exchange.

ABIDE IN LOVE

We must abide in His love. This is not a one-time deal, like once you get it, you move on. To abide in love means a perpetual returning to love. I have seen many people who started out on fire for Jesus, radical in their obedience and eager to give Him their all, but in a short period of time they faded out because they lost their current heart connection with the Person of the Holy Spirit.

People burn out not because they work too hard but because they work with the wrong motivation. When you work to get Jesus's attention or you are trying to earn something from Him, you will burn out. If you work to gain affirmation from people, you will burn out. We must continually return to the fountain of love and drink deeply if we are going to survive the turmoil of life, both the boredom and the busyness.

Many Christians who start their journey with the Lord full of great zeal end up feeling empty and disillusioned. They continually think there is something missing in their lives and wish they could fill the void. Throughout history a lot of very successful men and women in both the secular and religious arenas have reached the top of their success ladder only to go to bed at night in painful emptiness because they were not satisfied. They were longing for a genuine connection with someone or something that will fill that reservoir within, but no one and nothing can.

This is true, even in the lives of those who serve the Lord. On and on we go from one thing to another, trying to answer the longings of our hearts. Only the "superior pleasures of the gospel" can ever answer the longings of the heart, and only coming into contact with the living God will satisfy us. This is by design. This emptiness is meant to draw us to Him, because our primary life purpose is in Him.

I often hear ministers say that they are "burned out" or "disillusioned." They seem weary, empty, and sad, as though they are not spiritually alive. I am familiar with this feeling. I remember the first time I led worship in a large arena. It was a ten-thousand-member young adult conference. After I led the arena in worship, I walked off the stage and thought, "Really? This is it? This is the pinnacle of my life of ministry? This is what it feels like to do the will of God and to be used by Him?"

My ministry was at a peak. I was serving the Lord and people, but I felt depressed—not because I do not value impacting people, but I thought it would be more exhilarating and more satisfying than it was. The truth is, it is servanthood. No matter the size of the congregation or area of life you serve, there will be no satisfaction in that alone. The satisfaction comes by knowing Jesus's eyes are on you and connecting with His Spirit who is in you. This is the power of life, not the impact. Impact is good, but it is not good enough. Intimacy with Jesus, through the Holy Spirit on a regular basis and through the bread of the Scripture, is the sustaining power of our lives, not impacting people.

We will impact people, we will serve and labor in Jesus's vineyard, and we will work together with others to see the great harvest of souls brought to Jesus. These things are very good and essential. However, when we think that the sphere of our influence and the measure of our impact are where we are satisfied, we quickly learn how empty they are. This is by design, because He never wanted us to just use us as a workforce. He wants us. He wants to be with us, to be in fellowship with us, to talk with us, to tell us His heart, and to share His thoughts and the deep things (1 Cor. 2:10–12). He is a bridegroom at the core of His personality, and He wants our hearts in the midst of our service.

MATTHEW 25

In Matthew 25:1–13 Jesus tells a parable about the Bridegroom God and the ten virgins.

> The kingdom of heaven shall be likened to ten virgins who took their lamps and went out to meet the bridegroom. Now five of them were wise, and five were foolish. Those who were foolish took their lamps and took no oil with them, but the wise took oil in their vessels with their lamps. But while the bridegroom was delayed, they all slumbered and slept. And at midnight a cry was heard: "Behold, the bridegroom is coming; go out to meet him!"...And the foolish said to the wise, "Give us some of your oil, for our lamps are going out." But the wise answered, saying, "No, lest there should not be enough for us and you; but go rather to those who sell, and buy for yourselves."....Watch therefore, for you know neither the day nor the hour in which the Son of Man is coming.

All ten of them had lamps. They were preparing for the upcoming wedding. We know all ten of them represent the redeemed because they are all called "virgins." We know they specifically represent people who have ministries because they all have lamps. They represent people who love the Bridegroom, have reordered their lives in order to find Him, and have been used to bring others to Him. They represent ministers who at one time had a vibrant connection with the Bridegroom. The challenge is keeping the oil in the lamp in the midst of the busyness of shining. Some get preoccupied with running around and gathering a crowd, and they forget that the only thing that is keeping them shining is the internal reality of the oil within, the oil of the Holy Spirit. It is the secret life in God.

Everyone sleeps (Matt. 25:5)

These ten ministers had a connection with the Bridegroom. They had a genuine desire to bring people to Jesus, but over time something happens. The hour gets late and everyone sleeps. Notice, everyone sleeps, not just the foolish. These ministers were preaching on the Bridegroom and telling about His coming. But there is a delay, and in the delay they all slept.

Sleep, in this passage, is not negative, but it speaks of the routine of life. We all have mundane routineness in our lives, even while we are waiting for the breaking in of the Bridegroom. What we do with our hearts in this delay defines wisdom and folly (vv. 2–4). All ten of them slept.

This is a reality that came at me hard when I was young. I quickly found that even life in God has an element of routine. Sometimes it is boring and mundane. This is all part of His design for humans living in a fallen world. At first it really threw me off, but over time I have learned to go with the ebb and flow of life with Him.

They all slept, but there was a divide happening in the camp. Here, in this one passage, Jesus Himself defines wisdom and folly. We know, if Jesus is telling us how He defines wisdom and foolishness, we better pay close attention. This is the same Man who is going to evaluate our lives in the end, so what He is saying here in this passage is not just a helpful hint; it is also a crucial defining statement about what He is looking for and therefore what we are looking for. Again, we will only be satisfied in satisfying Him, and here He is telling us what that is.

Midnight cry (Matt. 25:6)

At the midnight hour a cry is heard, "Behold the Bridegroom! Go out to meet Him!" I believe this ultimately speaks of the second coming of Jesus, but it also speaks of the waves of revival that will happen between now and then. When this shout is heard, the entire camp scurries around, discombobulated by being awakened from their deep sleep. They are in the darkest part of the night. This is the defining moment. The problem wasn't that they slept; the problem was five of them had no oil, and they didn't realize it until it was too late.

These five had been so preoccupied with their lamps

and running around networking, building, and being busy that they neglected their relationship with God Himself. They had become like the church of Ephesus who left their first love (Rev. 2:4). They became preoccupied with their impact instead of being preoccupied with Jesus Himself, and they did not have oil. The oil speaks of the heart connection with Jesus through the Holy Spirit. Some assume that once they have it, they always have it, and they take for granted their lives of prayer and their ability to connect with Jesus.

Little by little, if you lose hold of this, before you know it, you rarely talk to Him, though you talk about Him, and you rarely are with Him, though you are working hard for Him. Jesus calls this foolishness (Matt. 25:3). It is foolish because we were designed by Him to be with Him. How foolish it is to only talk about Him but to neglect taking the time to be close to Him? What are we persuading men into if we ourselves are not in vibrant relationship with Jesus? Christianity isn't a "do-good club." It is a relationship with a real person, and when we are beckoning people to come to Him, we are not asking them to join a club and do good deeds; we are asking them to come to a person because of His great love for them. We cannot bring others where we do not go.

When the midnight cry went out, these foolish ones had the shock of their lives. They had a name that they were alive, but they were dead on the inside (Rev. 3:1). They had a reputation of knowing God, but they did not have a current, living relationship with Him. I believe they were saved but had no oil in their lamps. Lamps represent ministries.

In the generation that the Lord returns, I believe we will see many who once had ministries that will then be burned out and no longer effective. They will have gotten so caught up in the busyness of ministry that they forgot to stay connected to the vine; therefore they will no longer have oil. This is a frightening reality to me, and one that I take very personally. Not only is it about public ministry, but it is also about life purpose. Many lose sight of their life purpose in connecting with God and get busy with whatever is in front of them.

Maybe your ministry assignment is in the marketplace, with your family, or your neighborhood. Whatever the sphere, once you become more preoccupied with doing the work of Jesus than connecting with Jesus, you become foolish. Yes, we must do the work, but it must be because of an overflow of encountering Jesus at the heart level. He will often shake our lives in order to get our attention and draw us back to Himself. He wants our hearts, and He wants relationship with us.

Dream about getting oil (Matt. 25:4)

The five who were wise had oil. They had stayed connected to the vine in an authentic way. They had a current life in God, not just the memory of it. Oh, how this pains me at times! I remember a few years into my time at the International House of Prayer, I had been leading worship, building the house of prayer, and serving in the ministry here. I had started off with the intention of going deep in God and had consecrated myself to live in undistracted devotion, but my heart was growing dull and distracted. I remember it so vividly. It was late at night, and I was on my knees asking the Lord what was wrong and why I could not sense His presence. My ministry was growing, IHOP-KC was growing, but I felt farther away from Jesus than I had in years.

It was alerting to me. I didn't feel His presence when I read the Bible. When I sang, I often felt empty. I didn't wake up thinking about Him or go to bed talking to Him. I was living in a frenzy of activity, becoming a slave of the urgent and doing it all in the name of service. I thought I was doing what was right, but my heart was getting more and more dull and distant.

This is a frightening place to be in because when my heart is dull, I am much more prone to temptation and sin. With a dull heart I am not safe. When my heart is not alive, I am prone to depression and frustration that lead to more disillusionment and burnout.

When you do the work of the kingdom without being connected to the King, you will burn out. It is inevitable. It is Jesus's jealousy that is like a flashing neon sign saying, "Come to Me! Come to Me!" He draws us with dullness in the same way that physical pain alerts us to the fact that something is wrong in our bodies. When we are spiritually dull, it is supposed to alert us that something is wrong.

I believe the Lord can occasionally give us dreams that give us a picture or an impression that will give insight into our own hearts, so I asked the Lord to give me a dream and tell me where I was and how I got there. I must add, I have often asked this and didn't get a dream at all, but this night the Holy Spirit answered me in this way. That night I dreamt I was in my car, in the middle of a very, very dark night. It was pitch black, and I was on an elevated highway that was more like a roller coaster than a real highway. It had many sharp turns and quick drops. I was going so fast that I felt out of control. I could see only the road directly in front of me, and I felt panicky as I was speeding down this elevated highway.

Suddenly my car starts to shake and rumble. I think to myself, "Oh no, I cannot wreck this car. I haven't even paid for it yet." I look at my dash and there is a huge, flashing oil lamp. It is flashing over and over, "Get oil! Get oil!"

I immediately woke up and knew exactly what God was saying to me. He was answering my question of why I could not feel His presence. He was telling me I needed to slow down and get oil, even if it looked like my ministry was not moving as fast. It was more important for me to connect with Him than to have a fast-paced ministry.

We must never disconnect from the body of Christ or

stop serving, but we must readjust our hearts and take more time to connect with Jesus in the midst of our service.

In my busyness I had forgotten my heart connection with the Lord, and even in leading the house of prayer, I prayed too little. This dream was like an arrow in my heart, because I had hoped I was one of the "wise." Jesus was warning me, telling me that I too had lost my way, like the foolish virgins, and that it was urgent for me to reconnect with Him. I had lost my heart connection with Jesus and was on my way to a collision.

I believe we have these defining moments several times in our lives and that staying connected to God is a lifelong vision that must be renewed time and time again.

Buy oil (Matt. 25:9)

In the parable Jesus goes on to tell us that in the midnight hour when the cry goes out, "Behold the Bridegroom is coming. Go out to meet Him!", the foolish look at the wise and say, "Give us some of your oil," but the answer is, "No...go rather to those who sell, and buy for yourselves." They cannot transfer their oil. We must go and buy oil for ourselves. It is what Jesus said when counseling the Laodicean church to buy gold refined by fire (Rev. 3:18).

We "buy" oil or gold by investing our time and energy. Time is life. I cannot stand in a prayer line and receive a deep life in God by someone laying hands on me. I cannot get it once and then never lose it. To have a deep life in God is like any other relationship; it must be cultivated and sustained. You are always either moving forward or going backward in your relationship with God. It is never static. We are fools to think it is. When the wise say to the foolish, "Go and buy oil," and Jesus says, "Go and buy gold refined," *buy* means "cultivate and take time." We do not earn gold or oil, but we must put ourselves in the position to receive it. If we do not do our part, He cannot do His.

Again, it takes God to love God. We must give Him space and time in order to get our hearts alive so we can fulfill our primary life calling, which is to love Him and be loved by Him. We have to take our cold hearts and put them before the flame of God, and little by little we will be transformed by the renewing of our minds (Rom. 12:2). This transformation changes everything about us. We will work with a very different spirit—"a lover will always outwork a worker." If we love first and cultivate a vibrant relationship with Jesus today, we do not have to worry about becoming lazy and neglecting the work. The closer we get to Him, the more zealous we become for His purposes. We cannot maintain this vibrancy without the help of the Holy Spirit

DESIGNED FOR GOD

How do we take our cold hearts and put them in front of the fire? How do we connect with the only person who can reach the void inside and bring us forth in love? Sometimes we assume God is only in the sky, far away, but He is living within. Jesus said we have to come "to Him" when we search His Word. It is not enough to be a student of the Bible or a person of action, doing many good deeds. If we are not deeply connected to Him, we are still not fulfilling our primary life purpose. We were created by God for God. Our very being was designed as a resting place for Him. This is the Creator's original design for us to be with Him.

It is stunning to me how our human frame was created. At the core of every person there is a sacred space reserved for God Himself. The inner life of the human is a severely neglected reality. From within you are defined, and what happens on the inside of you shapes what you do and how you live on the outside. It all starts in the center.

GARDEN

There's a place within,
    where no man can go,
    in the secret reservoir of the soul.
In Your jealousy, You've created me
    as a garden enclosed
    for You alone.
Here it's You and me alone, God.
You've hedged me in
    with skin
    all around me.
I'm a garden enclosed,
    a locked garden.

Life takes place
   behind the face,
   where it's You and me alone.
I don't want to waste my life,
   living on the outside.
I'm going to live from the inside out.
So, come into Your garden.[1]

God created humans with layers, and at the depths we are reserved for Him alone. No man can reach those depths. As I mentioned in a previous chapter, there is a world within every human. Each of you reading this book right now has a world within that no one can automatically know. You have feelings, thoughts, images, and conversation going on inside of you. Life takes place "behind the face." The majority of our lives are lived in our thoughts, our heart, and our soul. This is why three of the four ways that Jesus commanded and prophesied that we would love Him are internal and out of the sight of man. We have utterly underestimated the power of the mind, and we have criminally wasted the most sacred space in creation—the internal world.

Think about it. Most of your life you are either sitting quietly in your own thoughts, having perpetual conversation in your head, or you are asleep where you are deep in your own soul. You cannot turn the conversation off, and you cannot turn the images off. This is because you were created for prayer. Prayer is a dialogue with God and a meditation on Him, which involves words and pictures. Each of us is designed for God, and He has fashioned our hearts individually (Ps. 33:15). Only you can give Him your love. No one else can.

We will never be fulfilled or satisfied until we encounter God at the heart level, because by design this is what we were created for. It would be like a bird never flying for a human to never experience God. We were made to soar the heights of encounter. We will never be content with our feet on the ground. If we do great acts of service but don't have Him, we are empty.

The Holy Spirit is divine fire, the very being of God Himself, and we must continually encounter Him. "This is eternal life, that they may know You, the only true God, and Jesus Christ whom You have sent" (John 17:3). This is experiential knowledge. *Eternal life* here is not only speaking of quantity but quality. *Know* in this passage speaks of experience. There is a quality of life that He gives that is a literal encounter with the living God. It is not a metaphor or only symbolic. We must come into contact with God Himself, who is an all-consuming fire (Heb. 12:29).

> Set me as a seal upon your heart…for love is as strong as death…its flames are flames of fire, a most vehement flame.
> —SONG OF SOLOMON 8:6

Jesus commands us to set Him as a seal on our hearts. He urges us to cry out to know Him as the God of all-consuming love. We set Jesus on our hearts simply by asking Him for it with a spirit of faith and obedience. To set Jesus as the seal on our heart means to beckon His fiery presence to touch or seal our hearts. By the very definition of love we must invite Him. He will not force us into a relationship of voluntary love. He waits until we invite Him in the matters of our heart.

We can't live without a greater reality of Song of Solomon 8:6, because life is too lonely, empty, and aimless without a greater depth of the love of God. We must put this vision before our eyes over and over again. When God promises to write His name on us, this is in essence the same as putting His seal on us (Rev. 3:12; 22:4; Heb. 10:16). The theme of Song of Solomon 8:6 is God's commitment to supernaturally seal our hearts with His fiery love. This refers to the supernatural anointing of the Holy Spirit to love Jesus as the Father loves Him and to fellowship with the burning heart of the Trinity as our greatest prize and primary destiny.

God wants to release the anointing of love as a seal. This seal is the guarantee that we will be brought forth in love (Rom. 5:5; Eph. 1:13). His plan will not fail, and the first commandment will prevail. God will have a people in unity with Him, and He will help us to love Him in the way He loves us. Jesus prophesied over us by not only commanding that we love Him but also declaring that we *shall* surely love God with all our hearts. He will help us. We must intentionally pursue this anointing of the love until the first commandment is in first place in our lives and ministry (Matt. 22:37). To set Jesus as a seal on our hearts is to call on Him to visit us by His Spirit until the influences of His love are progressively imparted more and more to our mind, emotions, and ministry. We set Him on our heart over and over again.

There is a literal encounter we have with God when we commune with the Holy Spirit. It is not imaginative or just a metaphor. It is a literal contact with God Himself. I am not talking about perpetual ecstasy or unusual encounters that are "supernatural" in the way that we typically define supernatural. I believe we will have those encounters on occasion. But what I am talking about is a steady stream of fire that is God Himself being poured into our hearts (Rom. 5:5). That steady stream will become a raging torrent until we are one with that holy, pulsating heart of divine fire.

We cannot fathom what we have been invited into in the "fellowship of the burning heart," and the Holy Spirit is the guarantee that we will enter into the Creator's original intention by becoming one with Him in the baptism of fire (Luke 3:16). "Our God is a consuming fire" (Heb. 12:29). Notice this is an action word, and it implies a continual consuming. He doesn't look like fire, He doesn't "put on fire" or "use fire," He is fire. He is light, and every light that shines is a light that burns, and He is love (1 John 4:16). Our God is fire, light, and love. This is the essence of who He is. Who can dwell with everlasting burnings (Isa. 33:14)? Who can contain the fire of God?

Scripture says that Jesus longs to baptize us with fire (Luke 3:16). In the Upper Room they were given a down payment of this flame (Acts 2:1–4). The very essence of God is supernatural fire, and every heart is a furnace. His Word is the fuel, and His Spirit the flame.

HOLY SPIRIT

The Holy Spirit is the fire of God living in us, burning continuously. Jesus even said that it was better if He went back to heaven in order that the Father would send the Holy Spirit. He said it was better, because then He would be in us and we would be in Him, even as He is in the Father and the Father is in Him (John 14:10–11; 16:7).

Wow! What did those twelve young Jewish boys think about these shocking words? Jesus spent three and a half years walking with these twelve guys, living with them, and traveling with them. They were well acquainted with one another and loved one another deeply. They knew Jesus as their Messiah, the one that they had been waiting for, and they believed He was going to overturn Rome and take over Jerusalem at any point. They could see the momentum building as the multitudes began to follow Him. They saw the miracles, they heard His words, and they saw His interaction with the leaders of Israel. It was all culminating into what they thought would be the fulfillment of Scripture where the Son of David would take over the throne in Jerusalem and rule the world from that holy city. Arguing about who would be the greatest and who would sit at His right hand, the disciples began to make plans for the future. They were clueless to the great delay they were about to enter into. They didn't grasp that He had come to die.

Before arriving in Jerusalem, Jesus told them He would be killed in the city (Matt. 17:23; Mark 9:31). He told them He would fulfill what He came to do, and He came to die. Imagine the drama of this moment. The man they knew to be the Anointed One, the deliverer of Zion, the man they knew personally as friend was telling them He was about to die. They had hopes in Him as their future King, and they had love for Him as their dearest friend. These guys had walked with Him day after day and had grown accustomed to His words, His smiles, and the light in His eyes. They loved this man. He looked at them and said:

> Because I have said these things to you, sorrow has filled your heart. Nevertheless I tell you the truth. It is to your advantage that I go away; for if I do not go away, the Helper will not come to you; but if I depart, I will send Him to you.
>
> —JOHN 16:6–7

He also said:

> I will pray the Father, and He will give you
> another Helper, that He may abide with you
> forever—the Spirit of truth...He dwells with you
> and will be in you. I will not leave you orphans; I
> will come to you.
>
> —JOHN 14:16–18

Imagine your best friend looking at you and saying, "I am going to die, but it is good. Don't worry, because when I die my spirit will be in you, and we will actually be closer than we are now. We will be closer than me sitting in front of you talking, because I will be in you and you will be in me. We will be one." These young guys must have been utterly confused by His words.

Oh! I tread upon this sacred text with awe. I know I am only peering into the mere edges of what Jesus was saying. God living in humans! Humans living in God! What? Oh, beloved! Who are we? What is this treasure in the earthen vessel of you and me (2 Cor. 4:7)? Christ in us is the hope of glory (Col. 1:27). *Christ* means anointed; this is talking about Jesus's Spirit. Christ in me is the hope of glory. His presence in me is what transforms me into His image, which is the image of love and therefore my ultimate purpose and destiny.

I cannot transform myself. I need the aid of God and God Himself in me. The Potter is molding me into what He desires, which is love. All of life is a journey of transformation from a cold heart to a raging fire of love for Him. He gives us a little at a time, because we cannot contain much. But the Holy Spirit is the guarantee that the work will be completed and we will be brought forth in love: "You were sealed with the Holy Spirit of promise" (Eph. 1:13).

ABIDE IN THE VINE

The value of the gift of the indwelling Spirit cannot be exaggerated. The Holy Spirit is the most underestimated person. We have grown accustomed to language about Him, but rare is the man or woman who actually lives in Him and stays there. This is the thing that you must know: the Holy Spirit is a real person, and if you have come through the door of Jesus and accepted His sacrifice, you have been born again, or born of the Spirit. At this point the Holy Spirit was given to you and lives inside of you. It is not imaginative, it is not an analogy, but literally God Himself lives in you. He is Spirit and lives in your spirit. It is as though your spirit was empty and void, but when you received Jesus, the Holy Spirit came, and there was light in your spirit. It is a literal, creative work. A supernatural thing happened when the Spirit came to live in you. He is a real person, and the power of life is in talking to Him. You have all of the resource of God Himself living inside of you. We cannot fathom what happened when Jesus said that He would send the Spirit to be in us and that we would be in Him.

I remember the day that we were doing a "Worship With the Word" session here at IHOP-KC. This is a session where we take a passage of Scripture and sing through it, spontaneously developing it through prayer and song. It's like having a Bible study through song. We were singing around John 15:4–5: "Abide in Me, and I in you. As the branch cannot bear fruit of itself, unless it abides in the vine, neither can you, unless you abide in Me. I am the vine, you are the branches. He who abides in Me, and I in him, bears much fruit; for without Me you can do nothing." Mike Bickle was prayer leading that day. Before we went on stage, he told us how to interpret the text so that we could better understand it. He said, "Every time it says the word *abide* replace it with 'talk to,' and the passage will come more alive."

Abiding in the vine is not only talking to Him, but it is a large part of it. It's simple: "Talk to Me, and I will talk to You." You will not abide in the Spirit more than you talk to Him and listen to Him. Talking to the Holy Spirit, as a real person, is the power of Christianity. We need to get rid of anything that hinders this conversation. We are not just reciting memorized liturgy; we are talking to a real person. He knows everything. He will even speak to us about the most practical, basic things such as how we should live, our finances, and even our relationships. He is our friend in a literal way. This continual dialogue is the key to sustaining a life of prayer and therefore a life of connection with God, which is our ultimate destiny. Everything else falls into place when we keep this one thing the center.

We are meant to be men and women of the spirit, and when we fellowship with Him, we are fellowshipping with the power that transforms both us as individuals and society around us. I once heard a preacher say, "The chariot the Holy Spirit rides best in is the Word of God." We must never go out of the bounds of Scripture, but talk with the Holy Spirit and listen to Him. He will give ideas, impressions, pictures, and words. He doesn't typically speak aloud. Just be with Him.

TALK TO GOD

Prayer is the primary way we talk to God and He talks to us. There are several types of prayer. The two I focus on are intercession and devotional prayer. There is much to say on intercession, but I am focusing on the fire of love and therefore on the devotional aspect of our lives of prayer. If you take one thing from this book, this is the primary thing I pray you walk away with. I assure you, with confidence, if you do this one thing, all else will follow. If you connect with Jesus, you will fulfill your ultimate life purpose, and you will find your secondary life purpose and calling. You will not miss His will or miss your happiness if you do this one thing and walk it out through obedience. You will please Him.

I believe that the power of life is in conversation with God. It goes back to the garden and His original intention for man, where He is seen walking with them, talking openheartedly without shame (Gen. 3:8). Before the fall of man there were no hindrances between God and humans; there was no shame, sin, distraction, or doubt. It was, as He intended, perfect fellowship and openhearted communion. Since the cross Jesus has been restoring us to this original intention. One day He will restore the entire earth, but today He starts in the hearts of men.

So then how do we get the conversation started?

1. Faith

First come to Him, believing He is there. The key is believing that He is near. Jesus said that we have to come "to Him" when we search Scripture. It is not enough to be a student of the Bible or to be a person of action, doing many good deeds. If we are not deeply connected to Him, we are still not fulfilling our primary life purpose.

> Without faith it is impossible to please Him, for he who comes to God must believe that He is, and that He is a rewarder of those who diligently seek Him.
>
> —HEBREWS 11:6

We turn inward and believe that He is there. As simple as this sounds, it is a far greater struggle than meets the eye. Unbelief is the distraction that taunts me the most because God is so invisible. You cannot please Him if you do not believe He is there, and you must believe that He will reward those who diligently seek Him. You may not have an instant rush of faith or an exhilarating heart flow, but you must have confidence that if you stay with it, He will reward you not only in the age to come but also in this life. In time you will start to feel your heart come alive, and your understanding will gradually be enlightened.

2. Manage distractions

When you come to Him, do not panic when unbelief or distractions hit your mind. Remember the enemy is a liar, and his primary tactic is to make you think something is what it's not—like smoke and mirrors. He is trying to distract you, and one of the ways he can do that is by telling you God is not there or God is not listening. Do not get in frenzy when this happens.

In my earlier days I was very thrown off by distractions. I would freak out every time and end up in utter frustration, full of tears, storming out of my prayer closet, and brokenhearted because I could not see or tangibly feel God. I thought what He was asking me to do was impossible because my mind was too busy. I lived at the mercy of my imagination and thoughts. I often left my prayer times with deep feelings of defeat. But over time I learned to stay calm and pay no attention to unbelief or distractions by taking the reins of my mind and continually bringing it to the waters of the faith where I would drink of the Word and the Spirit and be washed. Gradually I was transformed by the renewing of my mind, but it took time.

Distractions are part of being human with a fallen nature. Your mind is a continual camera recording your days and then playing it back to you in various chronological order and random arrangements of images, words, sounds, and emotions. If we are going to become people deep in God, we must learn to control our minds instead of letting them control us. You are not at the mercy of your emotions or imagination. When you come to God, continually and calmly bring your attention back to Him again and again.

He is there, both externally and internally. I often close my eyes and picture the Holy Spirit like a fire in my spirit man. I picture that fire like the burning bush, and I speak directly to Him. Other times I paint the Revelation 4 throne scene in my mind's eye, and I picture the Father on the throne, shining like a jasper stone. I see the angels and the elders all around Him. I see Jesus at His right hand, interceding for me. I take my place beside Him or before Him, joining in the holy conversation.

You cannot turn off the images in your head. It is impossible, so you should take control of them instead of trying to overcome them. You cannot turn off the pictures, and you cannot silence the conversation. You have been given these tools for prayer, but you must learn to use them (within the bounds of Scripture).

Some religions teach you to go to nothing and to aim for silence, but this is emptiness and wasted space. You cannot empty yourself and focus only on "being." You have to have something to look at and someone you are talking to. Many people today are looking for a spirituality absent of Jesus. They are intrigued by meditation techniques that calm their inner lives, but I assure you, it leads to darkness. At best they will experience an emptiness that cannot be sustained.

Jesus is the only door to the Father, who is Spirit (John 10:7–9). If you try to get to the Father by calling Him the "supreme being," "light," "love," or whatever language you are using, or if you try to get to Him through meditation but refuse to go through the door of Jesus, you are a thief and a robber. Meditation without Jesus is a lie, and it will lead to darkness. You must come to Him in order to connect with Him. You are not turning inward to yourself, but you are turning inward to the Holy Spirit who is your escort into the deep things of Jesus's heart (1 Cor. 2:10–12).

There is only one door, and when we speak of deep prayer, you must start at the door of Jesus Himself. You are being transformed into His image, not an ethereal love that has no definition. You become what you behold; therefore you behold Jesus and will become like Him (2 Cor. 3:18). This is the purpose and goal of your life, and it starts in the place of prayer.

To behold Him you must believe He is there, and then you must stay and abide there, drawing your attention to Him again and again and interacting with Him. You are not just looking at a painting or a still image. Remember that Jesus sees you. He is searching your heart (Rev. 2:23). He is literally looking at you when you come to Him. Do not become an art connoisseur where you are just giving your opinion about a painting that was painted long ago, but get into the scene and interact with Him through His Spirit and Scripture.

3. Come to the Scripture

When I come to Him, I picture that fire within or I picture the throne. Then I begin to meditate on Scripture, and the conversation gets started. You must always stay within the bounds of the Bible, yet we know that we have barely skimmed the surface of that holy book. And we have barely been introduced to that holy heart. The Spirit within is eager to take us on this treasure hunt, tell us deep things, and pour supernatural love into our very frame.

It is a real exchange, not an imaginative one. We use our mind's eye, but the spiritual exchange is real. That fire is real, and we are meant to experience it. There is no greater feeling than when the love of God touches our hearts. It is God revealing God to us. One of the greatest gifts that has been given to us is the Bible. So often we accuse God of being silent, distant, and hard to figure out, yet He has laid Himself bare and opened His holy heart to us by giving us the "transcript of His soul."

I know many people who have signed up to pray. They shout and clap when the conference speaker gives them a rally call to go deep in God and to change the world through prayer. But when it comes time to actually praying, they rarely do. One reason they don't pray is because they don't know what to say once they are in front of God.

My prayer time used to go like this, "I love You. You

love me. OK...now what? Help me? Thank You..." I had no idea how to fill an hour with prayer, much less how to make it meaningful and enjoyable. When I was about twenty years old, someone taught me how to pray the Bible, and I am not exaggerating when I say it revolutionized my life.

The Scripture is living. It is as though it is a pulsating heart. It is the heart of God Himself. I often picture myself coming to Jesus in my mind's eye. His mouth is moving, but I cannot hear a word He is saying until I turn up the volume knob. The volume knob is the Bible. It is the language of His heart, and what you will come to discover is that it is the language of yours too. Praying the Bible is the most powerful thing on your mind. It will change you, because it is living and active. It will transform you, because it is powerful. It will renew you and wash you.

When you come to the Scripture in order to pray and have conversation with God, you approach it differently than if you were studying it or just trying to get the general flow of a book. You cannot speed read when you are meditating. The goal is not to see how much you can read but how deep you can go. If you are a beginner at prayer, start with the Gospels or the Book of Psalms. These books are the easiest to pray and have many on-ramps into sweet dialogue with Jesus.

Another good thing to do is to pray apostolic prayers since they are written as prayers. The apostolic prayers are the prayers of the apostles that are written in the New Testament. They are already directed to God and will give you language to know what to say when talking to Him.

- Prayer for revelation of Jesus's beauty that we might walk in our calling and destiny by God's power (Eph. 1:17–19)

- Prayer to receive the Spirit's power that Jesus's presence be manifest in us so we experience God's love (Eph. 3:16–19)

- Prayer for God's love to abound in us by the knowledge of God resulting in righteousness in our life (Phil. 1:9–11)

- Prayer to know God's will, to be fruitful in ministry and strengthened by intimacy with God (Col. 1:9–11)

- Prayer for unity in the church and to be filled with supernatural joy, peace, and hope (Rom. 15:5–6, 13)

- Prayer to be enriched by all the gifts of the Spirit, including powerful preaching and prophetic revelation (1 Cor. 1:5–8)

- Prayer for the release of grace to bring the church to maturity, especially to abound in love and holiness (1 Thess. 3:10–13)

- Prayer to be made worthy (prepared or made spiritually mature) to walk in the fullness of our destiny in God (2 Thess. 1:11–12)[2]

When you come to a passage of Scripture, be prepared to stay with it for a while. Always have a notepad or a computer where you can take notes easily. Although if you are like me and prone to compulsion and addictive behavior, I recommend you stick to a notepad during prayer instead of your computer. I tell you the truth, I have lost more prayer times because I impulsively kept checking e-mail, social media, and impulsively doing Internet searches under the name of "Bible study." My prayer time becomes "personal time" instead of actual prayer, and I end up disconnected from God. So if you are like me, be honest with yourself and stick to the old school way of pen and paper. You can always transfer it to your computer later.

For example, you come to the Psalm 23. Close your eyes and picture the Lord either on the throne or Holy Spirit within you. Sometimes I just picture Jesus sitting in front of me. Read the first verse, "The LORD is my shepherd; I shall not want." Pause and direct the words to Him, "You, are my shepherd." Stop and ask, "What does this mean that You are my shepherd?" The Holy Spirit is the teacher, and He is the counselor. He is eager to teach you. Then pause and meditate on that phrase, thinking of each word in the sentence.

When I do this, I start to put it in my own words, still directing it to Jesus, "Thank You that You are my keeper. You take care of me. You are guiding me. You are mine, and I belong to You. You tend my heart." I develop what it means and pray, quietly and slowly, directing the words to Him. Sometimes I do not even speak them aloud. I thank Him that He is this involved. I thank Him for the truth that is highlighted in this passage. Then I write down the phrases I am praying, and I feel them on my heart. Then I look right at Him and tell Him. I start to feel His presence as I talk to Him about Him.

When there is a scripture that is a command, talk to Jesus about it and set your heart to obey. When it is an exhortation, set your heart to believe it. Talk to Him about it. When it is confusing, ask questions.

Another way to meditate on Scripture is to put yourself in the scene. Take the passage where Jesus is washing the disciples' feet. Paint the picture in your mind. There you are at the table. You are Peter. You see Jesus stand up and prepare Himself like a servant. You are confused by what He is doing. Then He fills the basin with water, picks up a towel, kneels in front of the first guy, and begins to wash his feet! You are appalled! You can't imagine the God of all creation kneeling down and serving. Next He comes to you. There He is kneeling in front of you, as a servant. Your heart breaks because it seems wrong. You refuse to let Him serve you. The argument goes on, and He breaks your pride with His insistence that you let Him serve you or you will have nothing to do with Him. Now you are weeping because you wanted to earn something. You thought you had to come to Him clean, but here He is meeting you in the darkest places and demanding that you let Him love you there. On and on the story goes. When you put yourself in the scene, it is powerful on the heart.

Do not let your imagination run away with you, and do not trust your imagination over the written Word, but use your imagination to interact with the Scripture. God is the designer of your mind, and He designed you with the ability to visualize for a reason. As long as you stay within bounds of Scripture, you will encounter God here in the sacred space of your mind and your spirit.

I have had powerful times with the Lord by putting myself in the text. I saw myself as Peter refusing to let Jesus wash my feet. I saw myself as Mary wasting my inheritance on Him. I saw myself as the thief on the cross who deserves eternal hell looking into His eyes of mercy, through the blood that dripped through His eyelashes. I saw myself there when the tomb was empty.

The Word of God comes alive when you see yourself interacting with the Word Himself, Jesus. Jesus is the Word, and these stories about Him are revelations of His heart. They are given to us so that we know what He is like. Because He never changes, we know if He is this way with Peter, then He is this way with us. That is why we have these stories.

Oh, they are rich, and the Bible has a wealth of conversation material for the one we love. Though we are not literally at the table with Him, we are with Him in spirit, and the truths of these stories are real. Prayer is a real interaction with Jesus in real time. He is watching us, and in the Spirit He is with us. The exchange is real, not only imaginative, though the actual story is in our mind's eye. Jesus is more involved with us than we know.

Remember, you must believe He is there and that He is paying attention and talking to you if you are going to be pleasing to Him. Write down your thoughts and what you have learned from your meditation. You will be surprised how quickly an hour goes by, and you will find yourself wanting to spend more time with Him if you stay with it.

One of my goals is to go to bed meditating and to wake up in the Word. The way you go to bed meditating is by taking a scripture, maybe one or two sentences, and repeating it over and over slowly in your head, emphasizing a different word each time. I'll use Psalm 17:7 as an example: "Show Your marvelous lovingkindness by Your right hand." You would slowly say this in your mind, directing it to Jesus. The first time you say it, emphasize the word *show* and think about what it means for God to show you something. Then repeat the text again, this time emphasizing the word *Your*. Do each word until you fall asleep. You will be memorizing the scripture, and it will affect your dreams.

All too often, if you are like me, you fall asleep on your computer or in front of some kind of TV screen, watching randomness in order to "dial down." This is such a waste of time, and it hinders the dialogue between you and Jesus. We cannot take an hour a day in our devotional lives to try and start a fire if we spend the rest of our days and nights pouring water on the wood.

WAIT TO BE ESCORTED INTO THE HEART OF JESUS

When you are interacting with Jesus through His Word, give the Holy Spirit time. Wait. Ask Him to increase His presence. Acknowledge He is there. Ask Him to escort you into Jesus's heart. Wait on the Lord, and your strength will be renewed. Focus on the Spirit and commune with Him. He is literally there.

Sometimes you will experience Him in a more heightened way than others. The measure of experience is not up to us, once we do our part. If prayer is mostly dull or if we feel a lot, either way we take what He gives us, and we thank Him for it.

For more on this kind of prayer, I highly recommend these resources:

- "Fellowshipping With the Holy Spirit" by Mike Bickle (teaching series), www.mikebickle.org

- "The Power of a Focused Life" by Mike Bickle (teaching series), www.mikebickle.org

- *Celebration of Discipline* by Richard J. Foster

- *The Spirit of the Disciplines* by Dallas Willard

- *Experiencing the Depths of Jesus Christ* by Jeanne Guyon

- *Prayer* by Hans Urs von Balthasar

- *Fire Within* by Thomas Dubay

- *The Way of the Heart* by Henri Nouwen

WHERE THIS IS GOING

Where is this holy love taking us? It is moving us into the burning heart of God Himself. Our God is an all-consuming fire (Heb. 12:29). His name is Jealous (Exod. 34:14), and He never changes. He is not jealous because He is insecure, but because He is fiery love and wants to consume us. He is exclusive and gives all; therefore He wants all. The nature of fire is to consume. It cannot stay in one place. Either you are growing colder or hotter in love and devotion to Jesus.

Our lifelong journey is to stoke the flame by setting the

Holy Spirit on our hearts and by meditating on Jesus. Love is not passive. Love is passion. Love demands everything. When we desire to get rid of everything in our lives that hinders this love, this love will propel us into radical, life decisions that affect our internal and external lives. We love Him in this kind of abandonment because this is how He loves us.

We must look at Him, day and night, feast upon Him, and meditate and be obsessed with Jesus if we are ever going to live in the wholeheartedness we were created to live in.

If you want to become a fiery, abandoned man or woman of great faith and love, behold Jesus, and you will be transformed into His image. This is what you were created for. In pursuing this, you will fulfill your primary life purpose, which is to be conformed into the image of love, satisfying the heart of the Creator who Himself is love. But it will cost you everything. It's simple but costly.

7

AS DEMANDING AS THE GRAVE

THE FIRE OF love that is being poured into our hearts is transforming us and escorting us right into the heart of God's story. The Father is preparing a wedding for His Son (Matt. 22:2). Our ultimate purpose in life is to become the eternal companion for Jesus and a family for the Father. We live to become this and to bring as many people as possible to the wedding (Matt. 22:9).

For us to be "equally yoked" to Jesus in love, we must love as He loves. He loves with His all. He is the lamb slain before the foundation of the world, which means He was sacrificial love from eternity past. Sacrificial love was always in His heart, and He set His heart to be a sacrifice for fallen man. This is love: to pour out one's life for someone else. This is love: to live and die for someone else. It is the opposite of our self-centered mode of living.

Love is the opposite of being self-preoccupied. Love is

being occupied with someone else. Love is expressed the greatest in a sacrifice of one's self for the one he loves. Jesus Himself said, "Greater love has no one than this, than to lay down one's life for his friends" (John 15:13). He is talking about Himself and saying that His death was the greatest expression of love. Since His humility and death on the cross are the greatest expression of love, it is God's definition and therefore the image toward which we are moving as people who love Him.

We must never seek to pay the price for our sin, because He paid the price once and for all when He was crucified. Death no longer has dominion over us when we receive the gift of redemption. I am not talking about paying for salvation or earning His attention. I am talking about love's definition.

THE BRIDEGROOM MESSAGE

Throughout the Gospels we hear the voice of the Bridegroom, looking for a bride who will be equally yoked to Him in this kind of love. The Bridegroom message is beyond an emotional, sentimental worship song, although emotions are a significant part of love. Part of the Bridegroom message is knowing that He loves us in our weakness and enjoys the process of our maturing, but the Bridegroom message is incomplete without abandonment. The Bridegroom message is about His abandonment to us and our abandonment to Him in response. When He was rich, He became poor, giving all so we might share in His riches (2 Cor. 8:9).

The power is in the all. It is in holding nothing back, not in heart, body, word, or deed. The Bridegroom is the one who jealously wants our all, because He generously gave all. (See Philippians 2:6–8.) This is a beautiful truth that strikes the cords of the heart of one who loves. Paul the apostle describes the Bridegroom message like this: "For this reason a man shall leave his father...and be joined to his wife.... This is a great mystery, but I speak concerning Christ and the church" (Eph. 5:31–32).

He defined love as abandonment. Paul said that the Bridegroom message involves leaving to cleave in order to become one. He makes it clear that He is talking about Jesus and His church. Jesus left the riches of His Father's house and the glory He had with His Father to put on flesh. He allowed Himself to be confined by skin, and then walked on the earth in humility and restraint, in obedience to the Father. He is fully God, but as a man He committed His way to the Father and lived to do His will. He left His Father's house to cling to humanity in order to give the Father the family He desires and to obtain His eternal companion.

Until we see His great abandonment for us, we will never respond in equal abandonment. When we see the lengths that love went, it creates in us a response that wants to love in the same way. This means that we too must leave all our old ways to walk in oneness with Him.

Jesus said, "He who does not take his cross and follow after Me is not worthy of Me" (Matt. 10:38). This is the voice of the Bridegroom. He also said, "If anyone desires to come after Me, let him deny himself, and take up his cross daily, and follow Me" (Luke 9:23). When He looked at the rich young ruler, the Bible says that Jesus loved him and then said, "One thing you lack: Go your way, sell whatever you have and give to the poor, and you will have treasure in heaven; and come, take up the cross, and follow Me" (Mark 10:21). This is the voice of the Bridegroom beckoning. Jesus appealed to their desire to love Him. This kind of love is based on desire for God. It is more than receiving forgiveness, but it is the lifestyle for those who want to go all the way in love.

When I picture Jesus saying these words, I see light in His eyes, like the look in the eyes of a man in love who is saying, "Marry me?" To *marry* means leaving your old life and becoming one with another. It is entering into a covenantal partnership that leaves an old life for a new one. It is changing your name, your home, your future, and leaving the old in order to cling to Jesus in this way. He said, "If anyone comes to Me and does not hate his father and mother, wife and children, brothers and sisters, yes, and his own life also, he cannot be My disciple" (Luke 14:26). We know from the testimony of Scripture that this doesn't literally mean "hate" your family, but it means in comparison to the measure of love you have for Him, all other relationships are secondary.

Jesus wants to be our obsession. He has fire in His eyes and is eager to take us on an amazing journey of love. He says to count the cost before we start because it will cost us everything (Luke 14:27–29). He also said not to look back once we start: "And another also said, 'Lord, I will follow You, but let me first go and bid them farewell who are at my house.' But Jesus said to him, 'No one, having put his hand to the plow, and looking back, is fit for the kingdom of God'" (Luke 9:61–62).

When we receive Jesus as Savior, we also get Him as Husband (Hos. 2:16). This is invasive and exclusive. The cross is a covenant where Jesus hung, arms wide open, heart exposed, beckoning the world, saying, "Marry Me!" When we receive His forgiveness, we said yes. And it is not a one-sided thing. It's an exchange. He says, "What's yours is Mine, and what's Mine is yours."

The Father also defines the Bridegroom message as abandonment in Psalm 45. We know by comparing Psalm 45:6 with Hebrews 1:8 that this is the Father who is talking about Jesus as Messiah. This is a psalm about the royalty of Jesus. First the Father gives a stunning description of events related to Jesus's second coming when He will judge the earth for the sake of humility and righteousness (Ps. 45:3–5). He talks about Jesus's beauty and majesty, saying that the throne of Jesus will endure forever. He is the King of the universe, and, as a man, He will rule from Jerusalem (Isa. 2:3; Jer. 3:17; Matt. 5:35). It is a glorious passage on the majesty and beauty of Messiah.

Then right in the midst of this beautiful song the Father sings about Jesus, I can imagine the Father looking over the balcony of heaven, right at the heart of humanity, saying, "Do you want to know the secret to My Son's heart? This Man who holds the stars in place, who sits in the center of it all on His throne of glory…this Man who will rule all of the created order forever and the increase of His government will know no end…this Man who holds you together by the words of His mouth, He is fully God, yet fully a man. Do you want to know what He wants? Do you want to know what moves His heart and what He calls 'beautiful'?" He says, "Listen, O daughter, consider and incline your ear; forget your own people also, and your father's house; so the King will greatly desire your beauty" (Ps. 45:10–11).

Jesus greatly desires the man or the woman who lives abandoned to Him. This is what catches His eye and what moves His heart: people who hold nothing back in obedience, emotion, allegiance, and in every arena. He wants wholehearted abandonment because that is how He is. This is what Jesus calls beautiful. To be beautiful means to be attractive. It is what attracts Jesus. I am not talking about earning our salvation or favor. I am talking about the kind of people He wants to surround Himself with and the kind of people He calls friend. Like the twelve apostles who left everything to follow Him, these are the kind of people He wants to be around, because it is the kind of person He is.

Yes, it is shocking. He wants us to be in, all the way, without an escape hatch and without looking back. There is no other human relationship that can be used to demonstrate this kind of abandonment. You do not leave everything for your father or your brother, but you do for marriage. It has nothing to do with being male or female. It has to do with proximity to His heart and oneness with Him, like David, John the Beloved, and the apostle Paul, who left all to cling to Him.

There are times in our lives where He asks us to do extravagant things that even seem risky at first, but we were made for the exhilaration of this kind of wholeheartedness. He wants you to trust Him with everything, and that is why the lifestyle of the cross is so powerful. It is the lifestyle of leaning upon the invisible one. Men and women who do this wholeheartedly, holding nothing back, are like beacons in the night of the world. These men and women stand out in history as burning and shining lamps. These are the kind of people who touch the heart of Jesus and change the world.

SELF-DENIAL

If anyone desires to come after Me, let him deny himself, and take up his cross daily, and follow Me.

—LUKE 9:23

These are the words of Jesus, the Bridegroom Himself. In our Western culture, to deny oneself seems almost sacrilegious. It is often the "sacred cow" that people will never touch. Often people in the church and outside of the church think of denying yourself as horrifying and even wrong. Yet Jesus, as Creator and Bridegroom, is telling us that self-denial is the way to follow Him. He says we must take up a cross and deny ourselves. Remember, this is Love Himself talking, and this self-denial is based on our desire to be with Him. He knows the way our hearts work the best, and He knows the way to bring us forth in love.

We were made to live for someone bigger, someone greater, and something outside of ourselves. We want a purpose that exceeds our lives. We applaud noble men in movies who sacrifice their comfort for a cause. We cry over stories about people who fought to the death in order to gain victory or freedom for their countries. We love the romances of people who gave all for love. We clamor to stories of heroic virtue and mesmerizing sacrifice, but when it comes time to be what we admire, it's a whole different story.

It is the lifestyle of self-denial and wholehearted abandonment that is the lifestyle of love. Love cannot be defined any other way. Today loving God is often defined by what He can do for us or how comfortable He can make us. It is selfish, feel good, and centered around "me." God does many things for us, but we are most satisfied in satisfying Him. So when we give Him wholeheartedness, we are blessed, and it is good.

All of His blessings are good. We should love them! But we should want to be caught up in the one thing that we can give Him—our love expressed in a life poured out. We are His inheritance (Ps. 2:8), and we need to get caught up in being His. We are the prize that was before Him, and we want a walk that is worthy of this calling (2 Thess. 1:11).

PAUL

Paul said that he was crucified with Christ. He said, "I die daily" (1 Cor. 15:31). Paul lived the most selfless life, and this is what the Father was looking for in Psalm 45:10–11. This is what Jesus is drawn to and these are the people He calls friend. Paul said he was first in authority and last in privilege (1 Cor. 4:9; 12:28). He was a slave. He said he was a slave of Christ (Gal. 1:10). He saw himself bound to Jesus. All of His accomplishments, he thought of as rubbish (Phil. 3:8); he didn't even want to boast of them. Instead he boasted like this:

> I am more: in labors more abundant, in stripes above measure, in prisons more frequently, in deaths often. From the Jews five times I received forty stripes minus one. Three times I was beaten with rods; once I was stoned; three times I was shipwrecked; a night and a day I have been in

> the deep; in journeys often, in perils of waters, in perils of robbers, in perils of my own countrymen, in perils of the Gentiles, in perils in the city, in perils in the wilderness, in perils in the sea, in perils among false brethren; in weariness and toil, in sleeplessness often, in hunger and thirst, in fastings often, in cold and nakedness.
>
> —2 CORINTHIANS 11:23–27

He endured persecution for Jesus because of His love and abandonment to Him. Persecution and trial are not the only way to show abandonment to Jesus, but they are one way that many of His friends have laid down their lives for Him. For those of us who are not being persecuted, we have a different challenge. We have to find ways to express love through obedience, and it often involves denying aspects of our comfort and ease, even in the midst of great excess.

THE LIFESTYLE OF FASTING

How do we live a life of self-denial and love in a modern world? How we do this? Mike Bickle calls it "the fasted lifestyle" and has written a book titled *The Rewards of Fasting*, which explores some of the ways we can take up our cross here in the West.

Today in America and in most Western civilizations we live in a wealth of distractions with much ease and an abundance of wealth, food, pleasure, and comfort. Many of us have little comprehension what true sacrifice means. We struggle to give 10 percent in a tithe, and we live in fear of losing small comforts, but the Lord is going to challenge us in this, because it is an issue of trust, which is an aspect of love. To love Him, we trust Him. We want to voluntarily transfer our trust from our wealth and strength to His in order to encounter His mighty hand. Our pennies for His limitless resource; our tiny strength for His endless might—it's a beautiful exchange.

Voluntary Weakness

There are many ways that we live a lifestyle of fasting. We fast with the intention to express love while putting ourselves in position for the grace of God to receive an increased capacity for love. It's like we are increasing the space in our hearts and lives for God. Fasting includes fasting food and the areas of time, word, energy, money, and influence. So many dynamics happen psychologically, physically, emotionally, and relationally when we fast in these areas. The issue of fasting is nonnegotiable for all who want to grow spiritually in a dynamic way. God knows that there are human dynamics that happen in us, and if we don't fast, those dynamics won't happen. The great psychologist calls us to fast because He understands the human spirit. His command to fast in these areas is a statement about how the human heart works, not a statement about God trying to get us to be tough.

Some talk about fasting as if God is a stern master

warning us to pay the price and "get with it or else." No, the Lord is calling us to fast as the Creator and architect of the human spirit. He knows how we function, and He knows the dynamics that happen when we deny ourselves in these arenas. Many people don't buy into this, and they have very little spiritual maturity even after decades of walking with Jesus.

Jesus tells us that fasting is directly related to experiencing His presence (Matt. 9:15). It is about love. If we give ourselves to Him in this way, we can have a greater grace to love Him. We are going to heaven, but I want the anointing to love Him in this age to the full degree that God will give me. He says, "With the same measure you use, it will be measured to you; and to you who hear, more will be given" (Mark 4:24).

Jesus said to Paul, "My strength is made perfect in your weakness" (2 Cor. 12:9). How would you like to walk in perfected strength? He says, "You want it? Embrace weakness. Lay your strength aside, and you will experience more of My perfected strength in this age."

What Jesus is not saying is, "My strength is made perfect in your moral failure." He is not talking about sin. He is talking about the lifestyle of fasting. The weakness that Paul was embracing was preaching the gospel in a hostile area. The Lord was saying, "Paul, I am going to give you perfected strength, because you are laying down your strength in order to trust Me. I will return the strength to you." Paul said, "I boast in my weakness so that the power of God would increase in my experience." (See 2 Corinthians 12:9.) He is saying, "When I fast more and embrace voluntary weakness, I experience more power in this age."

When we live in a lifestyle of fasting, we experience God in power and in love to a far greater measure. There is no significant way forward without a lifestyle of fasting. I want more than the introductions of the faith; I want the deep things.

The greatest men of God all lived in a lifestyle of fasting—Moses, Elijah, John the Baptist, Paul the apostle, just to name a few. If you had seen them and didn't know they would soon be in the Bible, they wouldn't have looked important in the eyes of men. But these are the ones God called "great." John the Baptist was the greatest man ever born of a woman (Matt. 11:11), and he spent years in a lifestyle of fasting for a very short ministry. If he was in ministry today, he would be written off as a failure, but Jesus esteemed him highly.

Forget what everyone else is telling you. The standard of Scripture is the only standard to live by. Burn all of the bridges and look for ways to deny yourself. Take up your cross and follow Jesus. Go all the way.

I can't love God and deny myself, gritting my teeth the whole time. I need help, and the Spirit will help me in whatever measure I want. Instead of asking how much I can get away with and still go to heaven, I am asking the Holy Spirit, "How far will You let me go? How abandoned will You let me be?" I want to go all the way. I cry out for grace and supernatural help, and He gives it.

WHAT WOULD A MAN GIVE FOR LOVE?

Paul the apostle counted it all as loss for the upward call of knowing Christ: "I count all things loss for the excellence of the knowledge of Christ...for whom I have suffered the loss of all things, and count them as rubbish, that I may gain Christ..." (Phil. 3:8). He didn't want people to applaud him for his past accomplishments or even for His radical obedience to Jesus. He didn't see it as noble or lofty. It is what people who are filled with love do. It is what people who have seen the worth of Jesus do. Once you catch a glimpse of Jesus, your faith grows to where you actually believe the things you are saying, and your entire life is changed. Paul spoke of this love that will pay any price. He laid down his open doors of opportunity, he served in a rigorous way, he was persecuted for it, and he lost his comfort, but he didn't even think twice because he had seen the worth of Jesus.

In the same passage that speaks about putting Jesus like a seal on our hearts, the writer goes on to speak of love like this: "If a man would give for love all the wealth of his house, it would be utterly despised" (Song of Sol. 8:7). A man who loves would give all of the wealth of his house for the sake of love, and he would utterly despise the recognition as though he did something noble. Think about it. If a man had a child who was dying and there was a cure for that child's illness, but it would cost the father all of his savings, all of his property, and every financial security that man had, and he would have to move across the world in order to get a hold of this cure, he would do it, and we would applaud him. But he wouldn't feel noble. He would despise the recognition and say, "What? Noble? I love my child. To give up my wealth is nothing compared to being able to save my child."

This is how people in love live. What would we not give up in order to follow Jesus? There is nothing that compares to being with Him and pleasing Him. There is nothing that compares. It is about desire not nobility when a man or a woman gives up all to follow Him. Only people who cannot see the worth of Jesus cannot understand why a person would give everything to follow Him.

I need to see Him more clearly in order to be more abandoned. My lack of wholeheartedness is because of my lack of sight. I cry out for sight, so that I can see the beauty and worth of Jesus and then respond in extravagance. Jesus literally wants everything. The truth is, this is what you want too. The books and movies are filled with stories of people who have gone to extremes to express love. It is a story that is written on our hearts, and when we really live it, we feel most alive. The reward of love is found in possessing the ability to love. This is our primary created purpose, and when we have the capacity to love, as the Creator defines love, we are most satisfied and most fully alive. The highest reward of true love is found in possessing the love itself. The anointing to love God is our greatest reward. Those who are wealthy in love do not look at price tags. No sacrifice is comparable to what He gives us in His love.

"...OF WHOM THE WORLD IS NOT WORTHY" (HEB. 11:38)

Men or women who have this kind of faith and are convinced that Jesus is watching them make it their life aim to please Him and become radical in their desire and dedication. We live as strangers in this world (Heb. 11:13). We are pilgrims, not of this world, but going through it as ambassadors of another age. We are missionaries on a mission as "friends of the Bridegroom" to prepare the bride for the wedding. We are not here to build our castles in the sand or to make a name for ourselves. We are in constant motion, moving toward something that is yet to come. Life today is of extreme value, and much of what we do has continuity to the age to come. That is why life is powerful, but we are those who are anchored with a hope and a future not shaken by the rise and fall of what the world has to offer.

The economic crisis, coming persecution, chaos between social classes, godless politics, or corrupt governments of the world are not the end of the story. We want to impact these things in order to bring more people to their primary hope, which is yet in the future. We walk as pilgrims unattached to things of this world, not disinterested or uninvolved, but at the heart level we are free from the entanglement and snare of the fear of these things, because we know where we are going. The world is not worthy of men and women who live in this kind of faith (Heb. 11:38).

I want to join that great cloud of witnesses and run this race with endurance, being faithful to the end. In Hebrews 11 the men and women of faith were those who were anchored to another set of eyes and had their hopes on another homeland. We are not of this world. Though we love it, we are not of it. We must never forget this.

Throughout history there have been men and women who have exemplified this kind of faith and love. They have been shining lamps in the midst of a dark world. They have denied themselves, taken up their cross, and followed Jesus with hearts full of fire and love. They are rare men and women, but they are beautiful. They are beautiful to us, and they are beautiful to Jesus.

I think of men such as Francis of Assisi who was the son of a rich man and had all of the pleasure of life given to him. In his youth he loved to party and was really popular among his rich friends. Yet when he heard the words of Jesus telling him to sell all and follow Him, he actually did it! His father rejected him, his friends left him, and he took all of his wealth and walked away from it in order to follow Jesus. He became one of the most influential men of church history and lived a life of abandonment until he died.

Another man I think of is David Brainerd, the missionary to the Native Americans in the 1730s. He was a young man who got so hungry in his pursuit to be pleasing in the sight of the Lord that he ended up leaving the comforts of his life to serve as a missionary to American Indians.

There are many great men and women who are shining examples of love and abandonment for Jesus. We have a rich history of men and women who lived so devoted and wholehearted to Him, and we are from a long line of people who were rich in love for Jesus. What He is asking of us is not too hard. Men throughout history have proven that it not only can be done, but it is also the best way to live. We were created for this kind of love. We were made to go all the way and to live for someone other than ourselves.

CROSS DREAM

To further emphasize the need for a lifestyle that imitates the cross, I will tell you a dream I had in my early twenties that painted a vivid picture in my mind. It was one of the most powerful dreams I have ever had. In the dream I was a child in a moonlit graveyard. The gravestones in this cemetery were huge, and there was an open grave that was massive. I was dancing around this open grave. A man at the foot of the grave kept telling me, "You better be careful. You better be careful."

I was being careless and childishly dancing and

twirling. Suddenly I got too close to the edge of this open grave, and I fell in. My heart stopped then raced in panic and fear. (This dream was so real and vivid. I can feel the terror even now.) As I was falling, I grabbed ahold of the side of the grave. I could feel the grass roots breaking under my fingernails and could taste the dirt. I looked over my shoulder as I clung to the wall of this grave and saw nothing but blackness as the cold darkness of this grave was biting at my back. I was petrified. I was sober minded and focused. I had to use all of my strength to get out of this grave. With all of my might I began to climb. It was such a struggle, and it took all of the focus and energy I had. My clothes were being ripped, my face was smudged with mud, and my body ached as I pulled myself out of this grave. I barely made it, but I finally got to the top and pulled myself back onto the solid ground.

In the dream I stood up and was an adult. I was sober minded and determined. I walked to the head of this grave. The man at the foot of the grave was still there, and he was watching me. I was on a mission and knew what I had to do. I stood at the head of this grave and slowly began to extend my hands in the form of a cross. I was slow and deliberate. My heart had no fear but a calm joy. I did not have childishness anymore, but I had peace of heart and determination. Whenever my arms were stretched fully into the form of a cross, the man at the end of the grave pointed at me and shouted in anger, "Don't do that! It looks like you are being crucified!"

When he said this, I stood at the head of the grave, my arms outstretched and my body in the shape of a full cross, the Lord Himself came from behind me and stepped into me. I cannot describe the feeling or what happened. But I knew it was the Lord. I did not see Him. I just felt His presence step into me. When He stepped into me, suddenly I came off of the ground. I looked down, and I was clothed with bright light. Light was beaming from my hands, face, and feet. Light was all around. I looked at this massive graveyard, and all of the gravestones started to crash down to the ground as the open grave that I had fallen into was swallowed up and disappeared. I was coming off of the ground with light. The power of the Holy Spirit was like electricity all over my body and all through me. I was hovering above the cemetery as it was being swallowed into the ground and light was coming from within me.

I woke up, standing in the room with my arms extended like a cross, praying in the Spirit with God's power like electricity moving all around me. He spoke to me and said, "You will either die in your immaturity and sin, or you will die to yourself willingly and experience My power and light."

I want to become mature in love and not just live as a child. I want to be conformed into the image of love by denying myself, taking up my cross, and following Him. I want to be like Paul the apostle and count all else as nothing for the glory of knowing Christ. I want to embrace the way of the cross to a greater extent than I currently am, and I am continually asking Jesus to show me the way of love.

Death to self is a key to life in the Spirit. We must take up our cross and follow Him in order to come into unity with Him. It is in this unity that we come into our created purpose and the Creator's original intentions. He wants to be one with us in fellowship, but we must be conformed into His image. We want more than the introductions of faith and more than the introduction of love. We want to be bound to Him, one with Him in mature, holy love that has power in it. The Holy Spirit will not fail, and the Father will prepare a bride for His Son that will be equally yoked in abandonment and mature in love and faith. It takes faith to live radically, but God will have a people who will love Him as they are loved.

Jesus used the right words when He called us to a cross. Death to self requires spiritual violence (Matt. 11:12) that radically deals with my sin and selfishness. It requires a continual yielding to Him. We have been given the process of life in order to "work out" our salvation (Phil. 2:12). This means that we have a lifelong process of being conformed. Even in our weakness and even though we stumble many times, there is a love stronger than our failure. If we will turn to Him instead of running away from Him, He will help us.

This love is stronger than death itself and is as demanding as the grave (Song of Sol. 8:6). It demands everything and will remove all that gets in the way. We want to be one with that fire and not resist Him. We want to wholeheartedly embrace the flame. Throughout history this love has been proven through the lives of men and women who were burning and shining lamps. In the generation that the Lord returns, His worth and beauty will be seen, causing such a response from His people that the end-time church will be victorious in love. It's unstoppable. The waters of fear, shame, failure, greed, or even persecution and martyrdom will not quench the fire of love (Song of Sol. 8:7). It is love that will motivate and compel a great company of people to stay faithful to the end!

I want to be one with that holy burning heart even today. This is where I find my primary life purpose, in His eyes, caught up in Him. How far can we go? How abandoned can we be? How much grace will He empower us with in order to leave all to follow Him? I don't want to ask how much sin and compromise I can get away with and still get into heaven. I want to know the exhilaration of burning the bridges and paying my vows. Like Paul the apostle, John the Baptist, and Mary of Bethany, I want to express love to the fullest degree that the Lord will empower me to.

8

IF YOU DON'T QUIT, YOU WIN

O NCE THIS VISION lays hold of us and we get our primary life purpose clear, we sign up to live before His eyes, loving Him with abandonment and walking it out through loving others by becoming a servant of all. Then we have to take a deep breath and get ready for the marathon. We have great need of endurance. It is one thing to write the vision or talk it. It's another thing to walk it out for the entirety of our lives.

HEBREWS 11–12

The writer of Hebrews wrote about the need for endurance in his letter to the early believers who were being persecuted for their faith in Jesus. These Jewish believers were being put out of their communities, synagogues, and families for choosing allegiance to Jesus. The political and religious environment of the day was hostile toward believers, and by choosing Jesus they were literally giving up their lives.

When the Book of Hebrews was written, many of these believers had been following Jesus for some decades. They had taken their stand and given their hearts to Him, but some were growing weary in the process. After a few decades some of them started to draw back from their faith in Jesus. They were second-guessing their decision. I imagine they thought, "I don't know if He is really going to come back." When they said yes to Jesus, they were saying it through the paradigm of the Jewish Old Testament promises of Messiah. They were looking forward to a Messiah who was going to come to the earth, rule from Jerusalem, set up a kingdom, and take over the world. They said yes to this Messiah. Then there was a delay they did not expect.

Some of these believers wanted to draw back. They said, "Let's just go back to the way of our childhood. We can stay with our families and keep our social status. We do not want to lose our jobs or our lives. This is way too difficult. Who really knows if Jesus is the real thing or not? Who can tell? He is not even here anymore. They say He was resurrected from the dead, but who knows?"

The writer of Hebrews spends a large portion of the book telling them, "Once you have met the person behind the laws and the prophets, you cannot go back." The writer is persuading them that all of the Old Testament— everything Moses did, Abraham, all the Law, and all the prophets—was all about Jesus the whole time. When Jesus stepped onto the earth introducing Himself to them in the flesh, face-to-face, they did not have the option to go back anymore.

A person standing in the sun will cause a shadow of himself to be cast on the ground. The old covenant was a shadow. Jesus is standing there from all eternity past, and there is a shadow cast, an outline of the person. That is the old covenant. It is a shadow. It gave them a very dim picture of what God looked like. Throughout history the nation of Israel was supposed to be telling His story the whole time, even though it was just a whisper and a shadow. The Tabernacle, the sacrifices, the feasts…He says, "Those are about Me. You were supposed to be telling My story the whole time." Somewhere along the way they got confused and started thinking the shadow was it. The shadow became their story, and they lost contact with the person whose shadow was being cast.

The writer of Hebrews was saying, "The old covenant was a shadow of a real person." Moses saw a real tabernacle. When he set up that tent in the wilderness, it says he was doing it as a replica of what he saw (Heb. 8:5; 10:1). He must have seen the city. He saw the real tabernacle and shadowed it. Moses was a man of faith. He knew it wasn't primarily about the tent in the wilderness. That tabernacle was pointing to something else. It was always by faith, and it was always pointing to the greater, "the real," the person behind the shadow. The writer is trying to convince them through this letter that they cannot go back. He is not telling them to stop practicing Judaism or to stop being Jewish. He is saying, "Come all the way; come to Me." He says, "I am the fulfillment. It was all about Me the whole time."

When He came to Israel and was talking to them in the synagogue, He was saying to them, "If you had really understood Moses, you would know that it was Me that he was talking about" (John 5:45–47). There were a few who said yes to Him, and those few then started to waiver in their faith because of the persecution.

WE CANNOT GO BACK

Persecution is happening in many parts of the earth today, but in the West we cannot fully relate to what these believers are going through. Our challenge today is the challenge of distraction, boredom, anxiety, and fear. These are the things that weigh us down (Luke 21:34–36). We have a different tension. The application for these chapters for us today is different, but the truth is the same. Who do you say Jesus is (Matt. 16:15)? The issue is going to come down to Jesus.

At the end of the day it is going to come down to one man, and the entire earth is going to be obsessed with one man. It is going to come this: Who do you say that He is? What do you think He did? Is He the only way to God? Is He the only truth? Our temptation is not to go back to the old covenant, but our temptation is to go to humanism or universalism. Some think, "Maybe there is more than one way." Others are not tempted to give up the truth of salvation in Jesus, but they just give up pressing into the deeper things of His heart. Many in the body of Christ are in this category.

This passage in Hebrews applies to us too, those of us who are tempted to coast along and love Jesus from a distance. We give up our primary life purpose to love Him with all of our heart, soul, mind, and strength. We subtly lose faith that He is watching, and we stop living before His eyes. A little compromise sneaks in, and over time our hearts grow cold. We once had fiery devotion and were willing to give up all for Him, but now we are comfortable and complacent. We once had a life vision of knowing the deepest things He would give to us, but now we find ourselves rarely in prayer and even more rarely in the Scripture where those deep things are revealed. This is the struggle that we have today, and it is a dangerous place to be because once we start sliding backward, it is a gradual thing, and over time we lose our center. We might even lose our faith altogether.

WE HAVE NEED OF ENDURANCE

The temptation to quit is our greatest temptation. We are tempted to draw back in our diligent pursuit of a deeper life in Jesus, not because we are being persecuted but because we have love of other things that gradually takes over the sacred space of our lives. Often we have cares of this world that choke out the seed of the Word that took root early on in our relationship with Jesus (Luke 8:13–14). We sometimes get tired in the fight and want to quit pressing for wholeheartedness because it seems like too much effort. This causes us to slip from our primary life purpose, and over time we find ourselves in the dark.

The desire to quit is common, not just in Christianity but in all of life. How many times do you hear someone say, "I just want to quit"? They do not even know what they want to quit; they just want to quit pressing toward their goals. We have a propensity to want to check out, stop pressing, and just give up. All of us face this in different times of our lives for different reasons. Maybe it is the pain of disappointment, the fatigue of working and not getting credit for it, or being misunderstood and overlooked. Often it is just our raw, fleshly desire to indulge. We want to "check out" and "veg out." Some would prefer to watch movies all day. Others want to play video games, eat, daydream, or socialize. Some of these things are OK, but when done in excess they cause great damage. So much of the human race is ready to quit a lot of the time, weary and discouraged. It is not different in Christianity. I often hear my good friends say things such as, "Oh, I just can't do it anymore. I want to quit." I have had these same complaints in my own heart at times.

There is a weariness that comes with the rigors of life, and we have need of endurance. We have need of a greater endurance the longer we are alive. It doesn't get easier in the battle. Though we learn and grow and often the battleground is different, it is still a war, and we cannot get out of it.

Most of us are not being persecuted. I want to quit just because I am bored. That is enough to make me want to quit. What if I was really being persecuted? The Hebrew believers, in the time this letter was written, were being physically, financially, and emotionally persecuted. Many times our temptation is simply boredom! That is how weak and immature some of us are. I am looking at this passage in Hebrews and thinking, "I need endurance! I have such easy circumstances compared to many in the world, and I still want to quit? I live in a free country. I have a Bible in my own language. In fact, I have several Bibles. I have access to great teaching by godly men throughout history. I have access to much knowledge. I have great teachers, and I am in a good community of people who love Jesus. I have plenty of food, water, clothing, and transportation. I am comfortable. I have understanding of my life purpose and have been given all of the tools I need in order to walk it out. If I am tempted to give up now, how will I survive when great shaking comes? I have need of endurance!"

We have need of endurance in the day of boredom, and we have need of endurance in the great shaking that is coming. There is a great shaking that is going to come, and we must endure today and then. If we cannot endure the pressure that we are under now, we will not endure in that day. The Lord is giving us little tests, little by little, to strengthen us and to bring us into maturity. It is not in vain.

The writer of Hebrews looks at these believers, and he tells them, "You cannot draw back. You have need of endurance. You know the truth. Now follow through." Faith is believing. It is a set of beliefs that result in follow-through. Faith and faithfulness go hand in hand. We are called to be faithful and to follow through on what we believe decade after decade after decade—not just a summer, not just in Bible school, not for a few radical years of our lives, but decades. The scripture says, "If anyone draws back, My soul has no delight in him" (Heb. 10:38). If we have made it our life goal to be pleasing in His sight (2 Cor. 5:9), we first have to believe that He is really there and watching. Then we have to believe He will reward us, and finally we must be diligent and persevere in seeking.

THE GREAT CLOUD OF WITNESSES

Hebrews 11 is that great hall of fame of the faithful. I love to read it every now and then when I get discouraged or full of self-pity. I pick up Hebrews 11 where it lists one man or woman after the other who endured faithfully to the end because they had a vision of something greater than just this moment.

One of the biggest issue with faith is what I see right now and what I believe for the future—what I see right now and where I believe I am going. Faith presses the limits of my heart to go: "I know that there is more to life than this. There is more to life than just the mundane, than the routine. There is more to life than what I see. This moment has significance because someone is watching me, and it matters. There is a real city where I am going, and there are rewards with glory and garments of light. I am going somewhere. I am passing through this life as a missionary and an ambassador, but I am not pitching my tent and staying here. Life, as I know it, is not 'it.'" The great men and women of faith had their foreheads set like flint. They were on a journey. Their self-identification was, "I am a pilgrim. I am a stranger in this life." (See 1 Peter 2:11.)

Have you caught a glimpse of that city that you are going to? Honestly, I have barely caught a glimpse. It is effort for me sometimes. Mike Bickle says, "If you do not think rightly of heaven, you will not think often of heaven."

I need a greater revelation of what is coming. I have to remind myself that I am going somewhere and this world is not my home. I work at faith and keep pulling my heart and realigning my soul. When I get weighted down with the cares of this life thinking, "This is as good as it is going to get," I have to lift up my eyes and set my mind on things above again and again.

These men and women of faith knew there was a city they were going to. They were not only looking forward to the Messiah, but they were also looking forward to a city. They caught a glimpse of a real location they were going toward, and therefore they identified themselves as citizens of that place and not of this world. It says in Hebrews 11:38 that "the world was not worthy" of them.

"By faith Noah...moved with godly fear, prepared an ark" (v. 7). For one hundred twenty years he persevered in faith. Are you kidding me? Building a boat for one hundred twenty years while preaching righteousness to sinful people who were mocking him? I find it hard to pray one hundred twenty days for something before I want to give up. This man was consistent. Faith is not just a moment of exhilaration. Faith is consistency. He was moved with godly fear, which means he knew God was watching him, and it caused him to be faithful and endure. By faith Abraham was waiting for the city that has foundations whose builder and maker is God (v. 10). He was wandering around in a wilderness. He was in the land, but he did not build the earthly city because he was looking for another city. He said, "I am a stranger here."

We are not "strangers" where we check out and forget about people, but we are pilgrims and missionaries. We are on a mission as ambassadors. I am an ambassador here to tell the world that there is more than meets the eye. There is more to life than this. I declare, "Do you want to come to the wedding? Do you want to come that glorious city?" We go to the highway. We go to the byways, to the rich and to the poor. We go to the good and the bad, and we say, "Come, come to the city. Come to the marriage. Come to the wedding. Come to the real thing." (See

Matthew 22:4.) This whole life is a shadow of the age to come. You are in the womb of tomorrow. You are in the womb of eternity. There is more to your life than this. This is important. This is crucial, but God is after something that is eternal. We go to the world, and we invite people to come to the wedding. We are here on a mission. This world, as we know it, is not our home. We are strangers in a foreign land. If you have been born again, you are a citizen of another country. I am looking for that city. I am looking for that homeland. I am looking for that place, and I want to bring as many people as I can with me into that city.

SEEING THE ONE WHO IS INVISIBLE

By faith Moses forsook Egypt. (See Hebrews 11:23–29.) Sometimes in our culture we teach that faith equals money, comfort, healing, happiness, and prosperity. There is some truth in this: the timing is not always what we expect. Look what faith compelled Moses to do. He could have been in the palace in comfort and ease. He was the grandson of the pharaoh. He could have been there, lived life to the fullest, and said, "God has blessed me." Instead he identified with his God and his people, and he chose to suffer. Scripture says that he actually chose to suffer with his brethren and "he endured as seeing Him who is invisible" (v. 27). I love that phrase. He saw the One who is invisible, and because of that he said, "I would rather suffer with Your chosen people and endure a life of suffering knowing that You are watching me than have the pleasures of Egypt. You are invisible, but You are watching, and it matters and it counts. I would rather suffer in this age than to live in the king's palace and suffer in the age to come." He did the math. He knew he was going somewhere. And the Lord said, "That is faith. That is righteousness."

If you look at some of the things these men and women in Hebrews 11 endured, there were a lot of good things: they were mighty in battle, they had some of their dead raised, and they saw great miracles. Then it goes on to say that they were tortured, not accepting deliverance because they wanted a better resurrection. Some went through trials. Others were mocked. Some were whipped and beaten, chained and afflicted, and even killed. Some of them were tormented. They had good and bad. Sometimes the dead were raised, and sometimes the dead were not raised. They endured from every side. The world was not worthy of them.

The writer of Hebrews was looking at these men and women who were considering drawing back from the faith, and he said, "Do you really want to draw back?" Then he paints a picture of this great amphitheater filled with a multitude of men and women who had gone before them, who ran the race by faith. He says, "Look, it is possible. They did it. They were just like you. They had a nature just like yours (James 5:17). They were not superhuman. They were just like you. They did it by faith. You can do it too. You can do it!" He is painting this picture. "What I am asking you to do is not too hard for you. Look at that great cloud of witnesses!" He just lists them one after the other. "Look! Behold! You are from a line of people of faith who have gone before you."

We are not running this race with the people in our generation. I do not look to the left and to the right and say, "Well, I am doing pretty good. I am a little more radical than they are." No, I'm running with Moses, Abraham, and John the Beloved. I am running with Elijah and John the Baptist. These are the people I want to run with. Look at this great cloud of witnesses who endured, by faith, to the end.

RUN THE RACE

> Therefore we also, since we are surrounded by so great a cloud of witnesses, let us lay aside every weight, and the sin which so easily ensnares us, and let us run with endurance the race that is set before us.
>
> —HEBREWS 12:1

There are two ways these men and woman are witnesses. First, they witness by showing us it is possible, as though they are saying, "We did it! You can do it too!" Secondly, they are witnessing by watching. They are watching the generations through history, but there is one generation that is going to finish this race that was started six thousand years ago. It has been a relay race, and the baton has gone from one hand the next, from one generation to the next generation. As the baton of faith has been passed on, the name of Jesus has spread like a wild vine all across the entire world. There will be a generation that is going to finish the race, and I promise you, this race will be completed stronger than it began.

To the early Christians the writer of Hebrews says, "Look around at that great amphitheater. Do not look to your neighbor. Do not look to the left or the right. Do not compare yourself to yourselves. Look up! Look around. You are listed among the mighty. You are listed among the strong. You are listed among the noble and the faithful ones. Run the race! Look around at this great cloud of witnesses, and let us run with endurance!" Scripture says the same to us today.

LOOK TO JESUS

...looking unto Jesus, the author and finisher of our faith, who for the joy that was set before Him endured the cross, despising the shame, and has sat down at the right hand of the throne of God.
—HEBREWS 12:2

After seeing this list of all of these great men and women of faith, it is culminating in intensity. These Hebrew believers were leaning into the message now. They were starting to feel emboldened in their spirit. Then he says,

"Look at Jesus! Jesus is the author, the finisher of our faith who endured the cross for the joy that was set before Him."

Some people read this verse and think it means Jesus ran our race for us so now we can just be carried along. No, Jesus, as a man, stepped into the race, onto the track, and showed us how to run. Look at Jesus. Don't just glance at Him. Study Him. Meditate on Him. Get to know Him. Do you know what His life was like? How did He live before the Father? How did He live before man? How did He come and go? How did He find His identity? Where did He find His strength? What was His value system? To look at Jesus means to study Him and to feast on Him. Come to Him in the Scripture through the Spirit and look unto Him. He showed us the way to run. He did not run for us.

We are saved as a free gift, but this passage is not talking about salvation. It is talking about after we are saved and have need of endurance because we have a race to run. Look unto Jesus. Transcribe Him. Describe Him. Meditate on Him. Feast on Jesus day and night, night and day. Imitate Him until you become the very image of Him. He showed you how to run. He ran faithfully in obedience to the Father. He suffered but did not draw back. He did not quit, and He did not give up. It was because of the joy that was set in front of Him that He endured. In this same way you and I will endure.

The primary issue in perseverance is an ongoing faithfulness in small things with a humble spirit. For thirty-three years Jesus embraced endurance even before He went to the cross. The essence of perseverance is continuing to faithfully press into God and to serve Him in small things even in the face of frustrating circumstances or people resisting us. The perseverance of Jesus is expressed in His humility. He showed us the way of humility, and His goal is to fill the earth with voluntary love and humility that will continue forever.

Humility is the greatest virtue. It equips us to experience the greatest intimacy with Jesus because it is the way His heart moves. The only time Jesus described Himself was when He said that He was meek and lowly of heart (Matt. 11:29). He tells us to learn this from Him. His perseverance was not an issue of strength. We often think of perseverance as a strength competition. His perseverance was an issue of meekness and sticking with it to the end, and this is the issue in our race.

There are many passages in Scripture that talk about Jesus's perseverance and patience. He did not have to persevere as God because God has no obstacles, but as a man He persevered in patient endurance. The marvelous truth of Jesus's perseverance is set forth in Isaiah 49 where we catch a glimpse of the heart of this man and what motivated Him in endurance.

Jesus was hidden (Isa. 49:1–12). He was hidden even when He walked on the earth, and today He is hidden because most people do not recognize Him. He embraced smallness, and it shocked Isaiah. This gives us insight into

God's heart and what He is wanting from us. I wish I had pages and pages to write on the humility and servanthood of Jesus. It is one of my favorite subjects. I challenge you to do a study on this part of His personality as you feast upon Him. When we see His perseverance in small things, it causes us to love Him immensely and to want to imitate Him, giving Him the same kind of faithfulness He gave.

Paul prayed for the church in Thessalonica that their hearts would be directed into the patience of Christ (2 Thess. 3:5). The word *patience* is the same as perseverance here. The perseverance of Christ is not only about enduring the daily pressures and temptations. It not only means staying strong under the daily routine of smallness and the mundane when no one is supporting or affirming us. It means more. It means finishing our work and not quitting until the end.

Jesus said, "I finished the work. I did not quit. I went to the end of My last breath fulfilling the work I was sent to do." (See John 17:4.) Paul had this same vision to finish well. He said, "I finished with a good spirit." (See Acts 20:24.) A lot of believers turned against Paul, and at the end he said, "Believers throughout Asia have turned back, but I am going hard and not taking my cues by how people respond. I will go 100 percent to the end."

I want to finish in the face of weakness and smallness. My ministry might get big or small. I may have no money or a lot of money; either way I want to do my assignment faithfully to the end. The Scripture says we can lose what we have gained if we are not diligent to keep it (2 John 8). Jesus will talk to me about how I responded even to the last day of my life.

Jesus lived in hiddenness and endured smallness, and so will we. In Colossians 3:3–4 it says that our lives are hidden with Christ in God and that when He appears, then we appear. The glory of my life is hidden with Jesus. The glory of my destiny and the truth about my life and how God is moved by it, though it is weak, is hidden. The glory of our lives will not be revealed to us until the age to come. It is hidden until Jesus is manifest globally.

As fragile as our love and humility are, they are glorious to God, and He says, "I will show you how much it has moved Me. I will show you who you are." The person who doesn't get you the most is you. You have written yourself off. Jesus is moved by how you said yes. You might think it is stupid. The Lord says, "Don't. The glory of your life will be shown even to you on that day. Just stay steady."

Hebrews 11:6 is a powerful verse. It says, "Without faith it is impossible to please Him, for he who comes to God must believe that He is, and that He is a rewarder of those who diligently seek Him." You have to believe that He is, and you have to believe He responds and rewards. The essence of faith that causes faithfulness is confidence that God is watching you when nobody else is, even when things seem small and you are hardly impacting anyone, yet you are reaching God.

Our prayer time is sometimes boring. The Bible is often

confusing. At times there is no manifest presence of the Spirit on our hearts. The money is lacking, and we have needs. We are tired in body. Our family and friends are wagging their heads, but we do the will of God because we believe He is watching. We believe He is, and it moves Him. We believe it moves Him, and He will respond in His timing. This is the way Jesus did it! He is not asking us to do that which He did not do. He did it perfectly.

AUTHOR OF OUR FAITH

He is the author of faith. He is the one who came up with the idea. Sometimes I just look at life, and I look up to Him and think, "You really could have done this any way You wanted too. You could have saved us and then just instantly made us perfect. Why the process? Why the race after salvation?" Just save them, kill them, and take them to heaven is what I would have done. Yet His way is the way of process.

As the author of our faith He is the one who says, "I will take you through the fire. I am going take you through the storm. You are that lump of clay, and I am going press until you are formed into My image." It was His idea, and then He actually walked it out so He could be our High Priest who could sympathize with us (Heb. 4:15).

Look at Jesus. Meditate on Jesus. He did not run this race just as God. He ran this race as a man. That is why He is worthy. That is why we can look at Him and imitate Him. That is why He is our High Priest making intercession for us, because He did it as a man to show us how.

WEARY AND DISCOURAGED IN SOUL

> For consider Him who endured such hostility from sinners against Himself, lest you become weary and discouraged in your souls.
>
> —HEBREWS 12:3

The only way to combat the desire to quit is to keep our eyes on Jesus. I often feel weary and discouraged in my soul. I have a complaint in my heart, and I say, "I cannot do this. This is too hard. This whole pressing thing and running the race, I cannot do it. I want to coast for a little while. How about I just sit on the sideline and watch other people run. I am tired of the rigors of faith." I get weary and discouraged in my soul.

Discouragement and weariness are the two primary things that knock most people out of the race. He called it a race for a reason. A race implies that you have to exert some kind of energy. Jesus said it was "violent" (Matt. 11:12). Paul called it a fight (1 Tim. 1:18; 6:12). Whoever said when you are a Christian you just passively receive everything? It takes effort to receive. We do not earn anything. We are not trying to get in a room we are already in. But we are entangled and weighed down, and it takes effort to get rid of the distractions so that we can receive from God. It takes labor to enter into rest.

In Matthew 11:12 Jesus said, "the kingdom of heaven suffers violence, and the violent take it by force." Then a few verses later He looked up to heaven and prayed, "Thank You, Father, that even children can do this." (See verse 25.) After that He said the part that most people quote, "My yoke is easy and My burden is light" (v. 30).

I used to read that and wonder, "Is it violent or is it easy and light? What is He saying?" The violent part is getting into the yoke. The yoke is meekness, yet everything in us is arrogant. The violent part is to get the yoke of meekness on. Once you are in 100 percent and you are not holding part of yourself back, you will start to experience the ease. It is being halfhearted that is difficult. I *sort of* want to be righteous, but I *sort of* want to be wicked. There is this little part of me that hates wickedness except that one little part of darkness. The battle is often fought over that final 10 percent. That is the war. That is the fight. That is the race. You have to exert some energy if you want to run this race.

Trained Through Pressure

> ...do not despise the chastening of the LORD...for whom the LORD loves He chastens....If you endure chastening, God deals with you as sons....Now no chastening seems to be joyful for the present, but painful; nevertheless, afterward it yields the peaceable fruit of righteousness to those who have been trained by it.
>
> —HEBREWS 12:5–11

We are often trained through pressure. Pressure is not the only way we are fashioned, but it is one way. If you have a doctrine of God that doesn't include trials, you will be perplexed. Sometimes God will cause pressure in your life, and sometimes He relieves it. You do not really know which it is until later when looking back. He is after an eternal you. He knows the end of the story. He knows where you are going, and He knows the best way to form and fashion you. Sometimes that is through fire, and sometimes that is through pressure. It could be emotional, physical, financial, relational, or other kinds of pain. If we have a theology of God that doesn't include forming us through these trials, we will be offended.

Not only our personal lives but also the globe will experience great shaking at the hand of God (Hag. 2:7). He is more interested in creating you and forming and fashioning you into a meek person than He is in giving you what you think you want now (Matt. 5:5). He is doing this so that He can hand you the earth in the age to come. Remember you are a stranger here. You are going through life. You are on your way somewhere. He wants to form you and fashion you, making you ready for what He wants to give you in this age and in the age to come. If we lose sight of that, pressure is senseless and without meaning. We start to accuse Him, saying, "If You are so good, why did this happen? Where were You? If You are so powerful, why don't You intervene?" We start to accuse God instead of seeing His hand working in the midst of our battle.

There are many times that He will break in and bring a miraculous intervention that will stun us, and sometimes He won't.

I have had cancer twice. Once when I was nineteen, and then it came back seven years later. When I was nineteen, I wanted to know God as healer. I believed that God healed. I was reading John G. Lake and all these faith preachers, and I wanted to know Him as healer for myself. I was quoting the Scripture, and I was standing on it believing with all of my heart, but guess what? God did not miraculously heal me. I was nineteen, and I had to do chemotherapy and have several surgeries. I lost my hair and the whole thing. God was after something else.

I believe we should resist the devil and fight against all manner of darkness, which includes sickness. God doesn't cause these things, but there are times He allows them. We fight and stand, and then at the end of the day we have to look up to Him without offense and ask Him to mold our hearts in the midst of the battle. We pursue healing, provision, direction, and all of the benefits of His hand. We not only fight the fight of faith, but we must also let Him mold our hearts no matter the outcome in our circumstances.

Sometimes I get into a humanistic view of God that says His main purpose for my life is to make me healthy and happy now. As though right here, right now, I should be rich, happy, healthy, beautiful, and have everything I want. As if He owes me these things. If I think, "You are good and this is what good looks like to me," and do not see the bigger, eternal picture or the internal working of the Potter, I will end up offended. It is as though He could say, "Really? You want Me to leave you selfish, arrogant, full of your own agenda, egocentric, and in sin? Do you really want Me to leave you in that state, because I'm 'so good'? How about you do it My way and let Me form My love in you even if it means through pressure at times." (See Romans 5:3–5; James 1:2–4.)

I want to trust His leadership, because He has an agenda that is not my agenda, and He is far more interested in producing humility, meekness, and compassion in me. I have so much more compassion for sick people just because I have been through a little bit of sickness. I am not suggesting that we embrace sickness. I rebuke it and believe for healing to the end. We cannot predict God. But at the end of the day we have to deal with the fact that sometimes He heals, and sometimes there is a delay in that healing. This is true in many arenas of our lives, not just physical health. He trains us through pressure.

We all have different stories. We have different realms of pressure that we do not understand. We have to define God's goodness on His terms. He is so good that He will sometimes allow pressure to train us and press us into meekness. He is so kind and generous that there are times we get broken in order to come up humble and grateful, leaning on our beloved (Song of Sol. 8:5).

SHAKE IT OFF AND GET BACK IN THE RACE

> Therefore strengthen the hands which hang down, and the feeble knees, and make straight paths for your feet, so that what is lame may not be dislocated, but rather be healed.
>
> —HEBREWS 12:12–13

Having a wrong view of God and what He owes us or having a wrong view of how life should be can cause discouragement, lead to a broken walk, and then to bitterness of soul. This passage is painting a picture of a person slumped over with their hands hanging down in a defeated position. It is a picture of a person in self-pity. Feeble knees speak of fear. This is a person paralyzed with self-pity and fear, seeing himself as a victim. How often have I been in this posture with complaints in my heart: "God is rejecting me. I am neglected. People do not understand my pain. I am overlooked. I have been wounded. I am hurt. The church is mean to me. I am sick. I have no money."

On and on we go in a spirit of complaint. God does not buy into self-pity but rather tells us to strengthen ourselves. Shake it off and rise up. Self-pity is disgusting. The pain we experience is real, and He has great compassion on us, but self-pity is not the way out. It just goes in circles around and around. He says, "Stand up. Strengthen yourself."

"So that which is lame won't be dislocated." The

picture is of the person running the race and their leg gets dislocated. When you have a dislocated leg, you have to pull it back into place or else it will heal crooked. It is incredibly painful but so necessary. You can leave it dislocated and eventually get over the pain, but your walk will be with a limp. There are times in our lives where our walk has a break in it. It is caused by something that happened to us or something we did. Often wrong paradigms of God or life will cause a root of bitterness. There are many things that cause this hindrance, but we cannot ignore them if we are going to persevere in love to the end. Disappointment, relational pain, unforgiveness, covetousness, and many other issues cause this break to happen. Those little things will cause a hindrance in your race that will set you on the sidelines or cause you to quit prematurely.

BITTERNESS

> ...looking carefully lest you fall short of the grace of God; lest any root of bitterness springing up cause trouble, and by this many become defiled.
>
> —HEBREWS 12:15

Look careful lest you fall short of grace. Many have a doctrine of grace that would say, "My leg is broken. My arms are weak. I am feeble and afraid. God, You know that I am broken. Grace. Grace. Thank goodness for grace. Grace covers me in my brokenness." Then they just stay there defeated for decades!

No, you are falling short of grace. Grace is the power to stand up, to straighten your arms, and to fix what is broken in your walk. What He is asking us to do is not too difficult. It is not too hard. When we say, "I cannot do it," we are accusing God's character. We are saying that He is asking us to do something impossible and that He is too harsh and not good. No! He is not asking me to bear anything that He will not help me bear. He is not giving me a burden that is too heavy. He has not given you a life history that is too hard. He has not given you anything that is too heavy for you to bear.

Get up and run. Do not fall short of grace. Do not take grace in vain (2 Cor. 6:1). Grace is the power to run the race, to shake off the self-pity, shake off lethargy, shake off complacency, shake it off and get up and correct the broken leg, whatever the issue is, and run the race. You have need of endurance.

Be careful that bitterness does not spring up in your heart. Bitterness is so sneaky and rarely admits itself. Bitterness is cynicism and says things like, "I already tried that. I have been there and done that. I tried that radical thing when I was young. I was radical when I was a teenager, but you know, you kind of lose your zeal when you get older." That is bitterness, cynicism, skepticism, unbelief, the inability to stir yourself up again because you have "already tried it." These are sure signs of bitterness.

One of the primary ways I think we grow bitter is because of our own failures. We are so tired of failing. That is one of the quickest ways I grow bitter. I get tired of getting up and falling and sinning and having to resign and back up. I think, "I cannot do this." It is an accusation against God, even though it is directed toward myself. I am accusing Him of being too difficult. I think, "I cannot be holy. I am obviously going to sin, so I am just going give up. Holiness is too hard. I am too weak. I cannot do it." This is bitterness.

We must be very careful that we do not let bitterness spring up in our hearts, because many people get thrown off by this. It is the most common threat to the devout. As I am getting older, I watch the people around me get jaded. When we were young, we all signed up for this thing, but over time things got harder. The delay in the promises lasts longer. Our lives get more complicated. I have seen many who were devout in their youth or in their twenties but now unmovable in their thirties and forties. They are cynical. It is hard to get them motivated.

The longer you walk with the Lord, it actually gets harder and not easier. Some aspects get easier. A lot of times young people think that they have it bad because they are teenagers, and I think, "Wait until you are in your thirties." Then I say to myself, "Wait until you are in your sixties." When I see a sixty-year-old, seventy-year-old, eighty-year-old, or ninety-year-old fiery believer waking in the first commandment and fulfilling their life destiny in God, it is the most gorgeous reality. They did it! They are not bitter! They are still running. I admire men and women of faith who have endured for decades. That is not easy, because of bitterness. He says, "Be really, really careful that you do not get bitter."

PREPARED FOR THE GLOBAL PRESSURE (HEB. 12:25-29)

God is going to wake up a generation. Hebrews 12 says, "Once again I am going to shake everything." He instantly goes to the Great Tribulation. He starts to prophesy of a future generation that would be alive in the time Jesus returns. He is quoting Haggai. He is talking about the glory of the latter temple. He says, "I am going to shake everything, and you have received a kingdom that cannot be shaken." There will be a generation that will run this race with endurance and will finish stronger than the race began. He will do whatever it takes to make it happen. He is going to take the globe, shake it, and loose us from everything that gets in the way. He is going pry our fingers off of our distraction, our unbelief, and our humanism. He is going to shake everything.

The writer of Hebrews goes from personal to corporate to global. There is a global pressure coming, and we are forerunners. We are messengers who are trained in the furnace of personal affliction. If we will get the message, if we will go through the fire unoffended and through the blessing untainted, and if we learn about His heart and get a testimony of His faithfulness and kindness, then we might have something to say when He shakes everything globally.

THE ARROW

Jesus was the ultimate forerunner, and He was trained in hiddenness and pressure. Isaiah 49 says He was like a polished arrow hidden in the quiver of the Father (v. 2). In the same way He is forming us into vessels who will hit the mark. An arrow is made with the purpose of hitting a target. Each person is uniquely shaped by God as an arrow aimed at a specific target. We may never have a public ministry on a microphone. It is not about a platform, but it is about our words piercing the darkness in people's hearts. That is the plan. Jesus said, "I am in the shadow of God's hand. He is making Me a polished arrow, and He hid Me in His hand, in His quiver."

Each of us is being prepared like an arrow. He is preparing you like a polished arrow in the same way He prepared Jesus. The arrow starts as a piece of wood on a tree, and then the grueling process begins. The branch is cut from a tree, stripped of its leaves, the bark is torn off, and it is immersed in hot water. It is this gnarly, old, bent-up branch that has to be straightened. They straighten the branch by putting pegs at the ends of it, creating pressure, and over time it straightens little by little. It is grueling, and it takes time. In our lives today we feel like this gnarly, old bent-up branch that is being pulled and stretched, but if we endure, we will have something to say and hit our God-ordained mark in this life and in the life to come.

He says He is going to shake everything that can be shaken, and only the kingdom that cannot be touched will remain (Heb. 12:28). His kingdom primarily starts on the inside of our hearts—what is going on, on the other side of your face. What we do in the political, social, economic, and natural order when it is done in righteousness will also remain, but all else will be shaken. We need to get the five-year-olds ready. We need to look at the children and be honest with ourselves; we are not moving very fast, but we are going to try. We are going to "mend the broken leg," and we are going do our best to run in the grace of God. We are going to get a young generation ready for the return of the Lord because we want to give the Lamb what He is worthy of. He ran with endurance, and He wants a bride who is equally yoked in courage, love, and strength. It takes courage to run the race.

He will make sure this race is finished in glory. He is an all-consuming fire, and He wants all generations. He is saying, "I want you. I will do whatever it takes to get you. I am an all-consuming fire." (See Hebrews 12:29.) The chapter goes on to say that if the people in the old covenant were judged because they did not believe what Moses spoke, and they had to wander around the wilderness, how much more will we be judged if we do not rise to the occasion?

We have come to Mount Zion. We have come to a multitude of angels. We have come to a great cloud of witnesses, and most of all we have come to Jesus, the mediator of the covenant! He will empower us to love Him fully and to endure faithfully. Let us fight the fight of faith to the end. And let us prepare the children for what is about to hit the planet because He is about to shake everything. If you do not have a theology of God who is going to shake everything, you need to read your Bible. He is going to shake everything. This is New Testament, after Jesus was resurrected from the dead. He says, "I am going to shake everything." Therefore let us run with endurance.

To top it off, you have to read Hebrews chapter 13. The writer breaks it down really simply and explains what it means to run the race. He talks about brotherly love and godly marriages. He is very practical. Wholeheartedness is not hype, volume, or a personality trait. It is holiness. It is living from the inside out and living that way for the entirety of our lives. We are weak, and we are broken. We will stumble many times, and there are hurdles to jump in this race. All He asks is that we persevere in patience to the end. Don't give up. Don't give in. If you don't quit, you win.

9

THE END OF THE STORY

THE MOUNTAIN OF questions I have faced from my youth gets resolved only one question at a time. That mountain gets conquered as I see the bigger picture of what Jesus desires. The meanings behind life's perplexities are primarily found in His original created purpose of the human race. They are found in His eyes. Often the tensions are great and are not always easily resolved, but I am committed to a lifelong climb up that mountain. The journey has led me to glorious discoveries. I have had many tears of frustration and many tears of joy as I have made it my primary life purpose to search Him out and discover the knowledge of God, and therefore the meaning of life. The more I grow in the understanding of His desire and dream for humanity, the more my individual life begins to make sense in the midst of it. The pressure, pain, blessing, and all the paradoxes of life start to make more sense as I hear the voice of the Bridegroom, wanting a bride equally yoked in abandonment, love, and humility. (See Revelation 19:7.)

I want to be caught up in His story as the Holy Spirit pours that fire of love into my heart. I want to become preoccupied with being His inheritance and His reward (Eph. 1:18), knowing that in satisfying Him, I will be satisfied. The story is a stunning one, though not always ecstatic or euphoric. It is a steady unfolding of the most profound mysterious reality, and we are wrapped up in it.

We must know at least the broad strokes of the end of the story in order to understand where we are going. Aimlessness is lack of vision, and despair is often the result of the lack of purpose. Truly we can endure anything if we know it has significance.

Since the beginning of the world the Creator has been working on a plan. His plan will not fail. Throughout the ages Jesus has been moving toward something and has had a purpose that will be accomplished. As Creator He has a sure plan that will come to fullness, and we have not seen it yet. But even today we are each participating in the beginning stages of that dream. Life as we know it is not the end of the story. This is not "it," but this is part of it. This isn't "as good as it gets," but this is part of the process, and for six thousand years He has been working toward something. The end of the story must be kept in view in order to not lose heart in our individual journeys and to not lose hope when looking at the scope of human history.

The first two chapters of the Scriptures begin with a bride and a bridegroom in the Garden of Eden, and the last two chapters end with the bride and the Bridegroom in the garden of paradise (Gen. 1–2; Rev. 21–22). The story in between the first chapters of Genesis and the last chapters of Revelation is breathtaking and glorious in the mercy of God. It describes the heroes of faith who rose up and said yes in the grace of God, even in their weakness. It also includes the stories of those who refused the kindness of God and the tragedy that came because of this refusal.

At the end of the story in Revelation 21–22 the bride is in the garden of God communing with her Bridegroom. That is how the story ends. That is the destiny of the redeemed. Communing is not all we do, but it is our primary life purpose both now and forever. It is friendship with the Trinity. All else flows from this living, vibrant relationship. It is the secret place of power for Christ and the church in this age and in eternity. In the Book of Revelation we see that this age ends the same way it started—God with man. From the beginning He has made His intentions known, and we can see His story line culminating even in our world today.

We know that the story of humanity has a happy ending, but we also know that there is a great battle and war for the hearts of men that lead up to that happy ending. This battle will reach its fullness in the generation that the Lord returns. It will be a conflict between two houses of worship, because it will be a war fought for the passion of the human heart.

Scripture describes two global worship movements at the end of the age. Many in the nations will worship Jesus (Ps. 72:11), and many will worship the Antichrist (Rev. 13). Jesus will return to this earth and complete what He has started. His plan will not fail. The Father will have a family, and He will give Jesus a prepared, equally yoked bride (Rev. 19:7). Yet we know that the Scripture says that glorious day He has been waiting for is in the context of a great shaking as He transfers the affection and allegiance of the world from that which harms them to He who keeps them. This transfer doesn't happen easily because men love wickedness, and they love the lie (2 Thess. 2:10–11). Those who resist the kingdom of His love will be removed (see Matthew 13:30) because Jesus wants righteousness, beauty, and true peace to be on earth, even as it is in heaven (Matt. 6:10).

He wants to restore the world to the Garden of Eden reality. This includes the hearts of men, their physical bodies, creation itself, and the governments of the earth. He is coming as a king to set up a kingdom. He is coming as a judge to remove all that hinders love and to cleanse the earth of wickedness. And He is coming as a bridegroom to give those who love Him His name, His throne, and eternal access to His heart in unhindered communion.

This communion with His heart is already happening, in part, today. The kingdom of heaven starts within (Luke 17:20–21), yet one day it will also come in fullness in every sphere of society and creation. Today, for the most part, the kingdom is in the heart and in the church, although we see a measure of the kingdom's influencing in all aspects of society and culture. We see this in part, but there is coming a time when the kingdom will be on the earth in fullness. The work that we do today that is truly built on Jesus and His kingdom will not be shaken. The things that are built on humanism, greed, lies, wickedness, and sin will be shattered like a clay pot under a rod of iron in the hand of Jesus (Ps. 2:8–9; Heb. 12:26–28).

THE SHAKING

At His second coming Jesus will come as Bridegroom, King, and Judge. When He comes to judge the world, He is coming to remove all that hinders love, because as Creator He created this world for Himself and for His pleasure (Rev. 4:11). As we have seen, His desire is to be loved and to love. He wants a kingdom of love; therefore He must remove everything that gets in the way. Wicked men who are arrogant and resist Him will be cast into the lake of fire because He cannot let love be defiled.

Mike Bickle says, "Jesus will use the least severe means to reach the greatest number of people at the deepest level of love." When we read the Book of Revelation, it is hard to grasp that it is the least severe means needed to wake up the multitudes of the nations because we cannot comprehend where the earth is going if we remain in darkness.

Even before the day when He appears in the sky, the earth will enter into birth pains that will cause great shaking (Matt. 24:4–8). It doesn't take a prophet or a pessimist to see that we are at the beginning of this shaking even now. We could be many decades away from the appearing of Jesus, but even in these decades leading up to that time, we see the hand of the Potter taking the globe and shaking it, turning it upside down. There are several aspects to the shaking, and not all of it is directly from His hand, but it is ultimately under Jesus's control.

1. Creation's groan

One aspect of the shaking is creation's groan (Rom. 8:18–22). Since the fall of man creation has been groaning for the restoration of Eden and for Jesus to come to the earth and reverse the curse. Creation has been under the curse of sin, and much of the shaking that we see is a result of this groaning.

2. Man's sin

The second aspect of the shaking is man's sin. When the Lord gave the dominion of the earth to man, He literally gave it to them, and humans have had authority to make real decisions that affect the earth. Isaiah prophesied that men have tried to change the laws of nature and have resisted even the natural order that the Creator put in place (Isa. 24:5–6). God has allowed sinful men to freely act against His laws, but creation reacts to these decisions, and it causes the earth to reel to and fro like a drunk man under the weight of transgressions, tottering like a hut in the wind (Isa. 24:19–20). Man has chosen sin, and sin has blossomed with severe consequences that are the result of this distortion.

In the generation of the Lord's return man's sin will reach heights we cannot fathom (Dan. 8:23; 12:10; Rev. 14:18; 18:5). Sin is not ripe until it is acted out consistently with sinful deeds, and it will be ripe in the decades to come. We cannot fathom where this is going. One reason Jesus is letting it happen is so the true nature of man can be seen, and we will see His justice and His mercy in light of the truth of iniquity. We cannot rise up and accuse Adam for choosing sin and causing all men after him to fall. We cannot claim that God was too severe in His judgment of sin, because when we see the full-grown tree that began as a seed in Adam's heart, we will understand why God has such zeal against it. What seemed small to us, when looking at Adam eating of that tree and opening the door for sin in man, is a much greater crisis than meets the eye. It will blossom into such a tree of evil that we will understand the zeal of the Lord and will never again accuse Him of being too severe in His judgments.

It is also in the context of the sin of man reaching its fullness that those who are righteous will shine the brightest (Matt. 13:43). It is in the midst of this darkness and conflicting forces that the true love will be refined. We need the conflict and we need the fire (Mal. 3:1–6). It will be in the midst of the wheat and the tares growing side by side that the great harvest will come in. Men will see wickedness for what it really is, and they will want the light of righteousness—not all of them, but many of them. The darkness gets darker and the light gets brighter. The great harvest of souls will come into the kingdom at the same time that the harvest of sin matures. The wheat and the tares will mature together at the end of the age. (See Matthew 13:30.)

3. Satan's rage

The third aspect of this great shaking is Satan's rage. We know from the Book of Revelation that Satan has a sure end where He will be thrown into a prison and will no longer be free to act in the heavenly or earthly realm (Rev. 20:1–3). He is enraged at the idea of going to prison, and as we get closer to the appearing of Jesus, his fury will increase (Rev. 12:12). He will be cornered and will spew out all of the trickery, lies, deceit, and wickedness that he can. As his rage comes to fullness, he will try to execute a plan to keep Jesus from returning. The Old Testament prophets, New Testament apostles, and Jesus Himself gave us insight into some of his plans. But we also know that Jesus is ultimately in control, and Satan can do only what Jesus allows him to do. Satan is like a magician with smoke and mirrors. Jesus is not at all insecure about the coming increasing conflict with Satan.

He is looking forward to this day because it is the day where He will eradicate evil. This day of confrontation and vengeance is in His heart (Isa. 63:3–4).

Isaiah describes this time period. He shows how confident Jesus is concerning it. Jesus sits above the circle of the earth, inhabiting eternity, and looks down upon the nations who are raging against Him. They are just like little grasshoppers bouncing around (Isa. 40:22–24). He takes the ocean and measures it in the palm of His hand. He spreads the galaxies like a curtain. He is not intimidated by the nations, like a drop in the bucket, or by Satan, being the liar that he is (vv. 12–15).

In Psalm 2 the nations are seen raging against Him, infused by Satan. They don't want Him, His Father, Israel, or the Bible. They want to get rid of God, and they actually have the tenacity to war against Him, just as Lucifer did in his arrogance many years ago. It's the same lie working from the same liar, Satan. King David declared that God laughs at the idle threats against Him by the kings of the earth (v. 4). He laughs because it is a ludicrous ambition for grasshoppers to overcome their Creator.

Jesus is not intimidated by the rage Satan puts in the hearts of evil men. Though this rage of Satan will affect the earth for a short time, it will not end there. We will feel the shaking of Satan's rage, but he is already a defeated enemy (Eph. 1:20–22; Col. 2:15). Even if we lose our lives, we have the victory because death has been conquered. Though the rage of Satan will be intense and many believers will lose their lives in the midst of it, it will be this context that the great witnesses will come forth, loving not their lives even to death. They will overcome by the word of their testimony and by the blood of the Lamb, even to the end (Rev. 12:11).

4. God Himself

The final aspect of the shaking is God Himself. He wants to pry the fingers of the people of the world off of worthless things, and He wants to cause them to cling to Him, as they were created to be one with Him (1 Cor. 6:17). Today, in the Western church, as soon as you start talking about Jesus the Judge, people grimace and often don't want to talk about it. Or they have the wrong picture in their mind and think of His judgments in terms of His being angry with them, even though they are sincere believers. Others have theology that says He won't judge the earth, and I believe that these arguments need to be resolved by what the Scripture says.

As a Bridegroom who is the Creator, He has great zeal to bring forth humanity into their original created intent, and that is to be one with Him in the fellowship of the Trinity. He is zealous to remove all that gets in the way of this. He also has much patience and wants anyone who is willing to come to Him to come freely (2 Pet. 3:9). He has not made it too mysterious, but it is so simple that all who want Him can reach Him. Yet it is so simple that the arrogant never will, and He cannot let the wickedness prevail.

There are many reasons Jesus is coming as judge, and there are not simple answers to why He is shaking everything that can be shaken even before He appears, but we know that He is judging for the sake of righteousness, humility, and truth (Ps. 45:3–5). He is judging to bring down the proud and the haughty of the earth who oppress the poor, the widow, and the needy (Ps. 94). He died for love, and now He will fight for love.

We must be people who understand His heart and trust His leadership, not blindly but out of true agreement with Him. Think about it; what kind of God of love would let wicked men prevail and rise up to oppress those under them? What kind of God of love would let lies and darkness erode the world when He has the power to stop it? What kind of God of love would let perversion, murder, Satanism, demon worship, and all manner of evil go on and on without addressing it?

Even today there are more than one million women and young girls and boys each year being trafficked across international borders as sex slaves. They are oppressed and helpless. What kind of God of love will let this go on and on? What kind of God of truth would let people believe lies, even beautiful lies that look like unity, peace, and safety, when those same lies will lead them to eternal damnation? How can He not step in and address it while there is still time?

Oh, beloved, His judgments and the shaking that leads to them are great mercy and compassion. As Love Himself

He is pleading with humanity to come to Him, but many will choose the darkness and love the lie (2 Thess. 2:10).

He will bring an end to the wickedness of man. He will confront the greatest dictator and oppressor that the world has ever seen, the Antichrist. He will shatter all of the infrastructures that will have been permeated with the filth of the harlot Babylon that will have filled the earth (Rev. 17–18). He will rule with a rod of iron, and He will dash the wickedness of the nations and their kings who are against Him to pieces. He will rid the earth of wicked leaders, and in their places the meek will inherit the earth (Dan. 7:27; Matt. 5:5).

I realize that I am making several big statements that must be backed up in Scripture in a responsible and thorough way. This book is not meant to be a comprehensive thesis on Jesus the Judge. I am confident that anyone who seeks to understand what the Scripture says on this will find an abundance of passages that provide clarity on this important subject. I challenge you to search the Scripture, without any preconceived ideas, have an open heart and a sincere desire for truth, and ask the Holy Spirit to reveal the heart of the Bridegroom to you through His zeal as a judge. There are more than one hundred fifty chapters in the Bible that have the end times as their primary subject. If you would like this list of Bible passages, or if you want more resources on this subject, go to www.mikebickle.org. There you will find many free resources on these subjects that relate to Jesus as Bridegroom, King, and Judge.

MAN OF WAR

At His first coming Jesus was silent by comparison. He came as a Lamb to redeem the earth, and at His second coming He comes with a shout, as a Lion to finish what He has started (Isa. 42:13). There is a moment when the Father will commission the Son to return as a warrior King to use His mighty sword against the oppressors in the nations (Ps. 45:3; Rev. 19:15).

Psalm 45 is a most glorious passage of Messiah, and it is one of my favorites to meditate on, talk about, and to sing. It is the Father singing about the Son. The writer of the Book of Hebrews lets us know that behind the voice of the psalmist is the voice of the Father speaking to His Son (Heb. 1:8). This glorious psalm starts with the Father's heart overwhelmed and overflowing for Jesus (Ps. 45:1–2; Heb. 1:8). I think of it as the Father thundering from heaven, "This is My Beloved Son in whom I am well pleased!" The Father's heart overflows with His love for Jesus. This passage shows some of His emotion for His Son. I love it!

As the Father sings this song, the Holy Spirit will impart portions of it into the heart of the bride, who will join in as the angels look on. In this psalm the Father calls Jesus to action saying, "Gird Your sword upon Your thigh, O Mighty One, with Your glory and Your majesty. And in Your majesty ride prosperously because of truth, humility, and righteousness" (Ps. 45:3–4).

There is coming a day, yet in the future, where Jesus will

come as a mighty Man of War. On earth we will see Him as Bridegroom and will have hearts that are lovesick for Him, crying out, "Come! Lord Jesus! Come" (Rev. 22:17). We will be praying in unity around the globe, "Oh, that You would rend the heavens! That You would come down!" (Isa. 64:1–3). Jesus will be praying for the nations, and then when the scene is complete, the Father will commission Him to return. We see this coronation in Daniel 7 as Jesus is brought before the Ancient of Days and given the title deed of the earth and the action plan to cleanse it (vv. 9–14). We see the same scene in the Book of Revelation when Jesus takes the scroll at the Father's command (Rev. 5). In response to the bride crying for Him to come, He will return as a Man of War. He is serving the Father by executing this plan, and He is serving the bride as well as the world by cleansing the earth of evil. He is a servant at the core of His personality, and He is the same Man who came as a Lamb, with the same personality, yet this time He is seen as a servant King who fights.

Israel was looking for this Man of War at His first coming. They were looking for Messiah to come and eradicate the enemies of Israel, fight against Rome, and set up a kingdom in Jerusalem that would rule the world. They were looking for a Man of War who would cry out in the street and start a revolution. They were looking for a Messiah to fight for them and deliver them from oppression, returning Jerusalem to its former glory as in the days of David and fulfilling the prophecies of Isaiah and many others. They were not looking for a Savior or a sacrifice. They were not looking for a Lamb, and they did not see, even in their own prophets, that He would first come as a Lamb and then come as a Lion.

Today we have reversed it, and we resist the Man of War, but those prophecies that Israel was hanging onto in its day, though they had the timing wrong, are still true prophecies. He is coming as Messiah of Israel, as a Man of War, who paid the price for all nations, making a way as the perfect sacrificial Lamb for all of humanity to be restored to God. He brought salvation even to the Gentiles (Rom. 11:25–26), and when this gospel reaches the ends of the world, He will return as a Man of War (Matt. 24:14)

THE DAY OF THE LORD

For two thousand years, since the cross, resurrection, and ascension, Jesus has been in heaven praying before the Father and asking Him for the nations (Ps. 2:8–9; Heb. 7:25). He has been asking the Father to send forth the Holy Spirit to win the hearts of humanity to Himself (John 17:20–26). Throughout the centuries the Holy Spirit has eagerly been working, and He has spread the name of Jesus to the ends of the world. During this period of time the cynics, the arrogant, and those who "love the lie" and hate the truth have said, "See! He's dead! He was just a teacher, just a prophet, an eccentric man with a good message, but He was not God." The scoffers have laughed at the righteous throughout the ages and have mocked those who long for the appearing of Jesus by saying, "Where is the promise of His coming?" In the generation of Jesus's return, there will be many scoffers (2 Pet. 3:3–4).

It is true that no man knows the day or the hour or even the generation that the Lord is going to return, but one thing is certain; He is not a liar, and He will finish what He started—maybe in my lifetime, maybe not. Either way we are of the line of the great men and women of faith who have had this anchor of hope in their souls (Heb. 11). This anchor keeps us from wavering in the midst of the great delusion.

Jesus has patiently been praying before the Father, and the Father has been working along with the Spirit to convince the nations of the earth of the beauty and majesty of Jesus, their Savior and their Bridegroom. The Spirit has been convicting people of sin and righteousness (John 16:8), and the Father has been preparing the wedding (Matt. 22:2; Rev. 19:7). Together the Trinity has been working toward "the day of the Lord." The day of the Lord is both the day of His wedding and the day of His judgment (Rev. 19:1–10). It is the day of vengeance and the day of gladness (Isa. 63:4; Song of Sol. 3:11). "Woe to the enemy of the King on His wedding day."[1]

Jesus said that He would not return to the earth until all the nations hear "this gospel of the kingdom" (Matt. 24:14). He connected the timing of His return to the preaching of the gospel to all nations. Mission organizations project from statistical data that every people group and language on the earth will hear the gospel for the first time by 2025! Churches exist in all 232 nations and territories of the earth. The greatest harvest of souls in history is occurring now. The Bible has been translated in more than two thousand languages (used by 98 percent of the world's population). Wycliffe plans to have it translated in every language by 2025![2] This is a stunning sign of the time! Jesus's name has spread like a vine covering the earth.

He is the most beloved Man of all generations. There is no more famous Man. In the end there won't be a more hated Man. He will become the obsession of the earth. Men will either hate Him with great hatred or they will love Him with fiery devotion, but everyone will have to deal with Him. All tongues, tribes, nations, and people will choose Him or choose the lie.

In addition to saying that He would not return to the earth until "this gospel" reached the ends of the world, He also said He would not return to Jerusalem until the leaders of that city invite Him (Matt. 23:29). The Father is preparing a wedding for His Son, and that wedding will take place in Israel. There will be a remnant from the seed of Abraham, Jacob, and Isaac who will call on the name of Yeshua, with love, in the identity of a Bride. It will come to pass.

The stage for the end-time drama is Israel. The glory of Jesus the Messiah will be displayed on that great stage as the entire world watches. The end-time drama is about the knowledge of Jesus and the nations of the earth seeing the way He deals with Israel and knowing this is how He will deal with them too. Israel is the witness, and even when they don't want to be, they are the canvas on which His portrait is painted. We know Him through Israel's prophets and patriarchs, and we know Him through twelve Jewish men who walked with Him for three and a half years. He Himself is Jewish and has chosen that family line to make Himself known. All eyes will be on Jerusalem as Jesus takes the scroll and opens the seals (Rev. 5:7–9). Even before those final days we see the nations reacting to His plan. The conflict is great.

This conflict that is rising will be beyond anything seen in human history. As the events in the Book of Revelation unfold, there will be a deep darkness that will come over the earth like a wave of delusion at the same time God's glory will be released in an unprecedented way on His true church (Isa. 60:1–2). Yet we know that there will be a great falling away in the midst of this, even within the church, because deception and delusion will increase greatly (Matt. 24:9–13; 2 Thess. 2:3–11; 1 Tim. 4:1–2; 2 Tim. 3:1–7; 4:3–4). The delusion will include false peace and safety (1 Thess. 5:3), but it is absent of Jesus and therefore absent of truth.

Many who currently profess to be Christians will fall away while at the same time the greatest harvest in history comes into the kingdom. Those who love truth will run deeper into it; those who love the lie will go all the way into it. Malachi says that Jesus will come as a refiner's fire, and He will start in His temple (Mal. 3:1–6). Jeremiah prophesied of the shepherds who tell lies in God's name (Jer. 23). God will silence them by drawing a line in the sand where the gray areas will not be so gray.

Several years ago I was in a time of intercession, and I was crying out for America and for God to raise up leaders. I was crying out for mercy and asking for help. I suddenly felt the presence of the Lord strongly, and I heard His voice clearly. I have only heard His voice at this intensity a few times in my life. It stopped me in my tracks. He said, "What's it to you if I raise up a man like an ax in My hand to judge My church? They lie! They lie about Me. They lie about My deity. They lie about My humanity. They lie about My first coming, and they lie about My second coming! What's it to you if I judge My church?"

I was shattered to the core and terrified. I realized that one of the answers to my cry for mercy would be the exposure of the lies that are in the church. Not all of the church lies about Jesus. There are many who love Him and believe what He said about Himself. There are also many in the church who are wavering and tottering on the fence, looking over the edge and considering more ways to God than just Jesus, or maybe that Jesus wasn't really God. Some are saying He isn't returning to the earth. Others say He wasn't born of a virgin. On and on the lies go, and these lies are often perpetrated by so-called "shepherds" in the body of Christ. He is against these lies, and He will shake His house to expose them so that the humble, meek, and those who love the truth can see more clearly and run to His name and find refuge.

THE WORLDWIDE WORSHIP AND PRAYER MOVEMENT

In the midst of all of these conflicting ideas and the multiple factors that are creating chaos and confusion on the earth, there will be a people around the world who agree with Jesus and His leadership. They will love Him as He loves them, and they will be in the place of prayer and worship all around the world. There will be a song in the night that will awaken the dawn of His appearing (Isa. 24:14–16).

Isaiah prophesied of Jesus bringing justice to the earth. He emphasized various things that He would do at both His first and second coming (Isa. 42). In the middle of chapter 42 Isaiah paints a picture of a song and cry that will be heard across all the nations of the earth. He doesn't leave any area of the earth out. Even in Kedar, which is an Islamic village, this song will be heard! (See verse 11.)

Today the Holy Spirit is awakening this song. There will be a worldwide worship and prayer movement made up of the global body of Christ. Jesus will return in response to the love songs and the intercessory cry for justice (Luke 18:7–8).

In Isaiah 24 Isaiah paints the most vivid picture of the condition the world will be in at the Second Coming. As you read it, you feel dreadful and wonder if there is any hope. Suddenly right in the middle of that dark chapter he burst out with hope:

> They shall lift up their voice, they shall sing; for the majesty of the LORD they shall cry aloud from the sea. Therefore glorify the LORD in the dawning light, the name of the LORD God of Israel in the coastlands of the sea. From the ends of the earth we have heard songs: "Glory to the righteous!"
>
> —ISAIAH 24:14–16

The righteous are seen in the middle of the darkness, in the midst of tribulation, and in the shaking as burning and shining lamps, bringing a multitude to Him and pulling on the strings of His heart beckoning Him to return. This worldwide worship movement will see Him as a Bridegroom (Rev. 22:17), and the Holy Spirit will establish the first commandment to first place in the body of Christ. (See Ephesians 5:27.) This great company of people will not only be an army, a workforce, or the body alone, but they will also be the bride. They will sing songs of love and pray prayers of love because they genuinely have encountered the voice of the Bridegroom.

Isaiah informs us that the primary theme of the songs will be the majesty of the Lord (Isa. 24:14). This is the awestruck, beauty-filled, fear of the Lord. It is beauty. We sing of His glory and His majesty, and we sing of His love and His mercy. I believe one of the primary songs that will be sung will be the song of all songs as well as the hymns of Revelation that are full of majesty and adoration. Not only will we sing about majesty, but also the Lord will anoint this worship and prayer with His presence, and the majestic splendor of God's presence will be in the prayer rooms around the world, as the firstfruit of Jesus being on the earth. He will manifest His majesty, which will be seen through healing, signs and wonders, deliverance, and salvation as well as the evidence of the fear of the Lord and the supernatural capacity to love Him in great faith.

Oh, we are only at the beginning of the beginning of where this is going, but just as you see the edges of the dawn long before you see the sun, we will see the beams of His brilliance fill the prayer rooms of the world long before we see Him face-to-face. It is the first sign on the horizon that the sun is about to appear.

We want to be people who usher in that light because we have encountered Him and are carriers of His Spirit. It says in Daniel that the people of understanding will instruct many and the wise will shine like the stars (Dan. 12:3). It says of John the Baptist, at Jesus's first coming, that he was a burning and shining lamp. Jesus will raise up burning and shining lamps at His second coming too, and they will be men and women who have encountered the light and are filled with understanding and power.

FRIENDS OF THE BRIDEGROOM

Those who awaken the dawn of the millennium and the return of Jesus will be in profound agreement with His heart, because they will be the ones who have lived before the Audience of One, in a locked gaze with Jesus. They are the ones who have lived the Sermon on the Mount wholeheartedly, seeking to love Him with all of their heart, soul, mind, and strength. They are the ones who have lived lives of communion, sacrifice, and love for others. They have the fire of God poured into their hearts by the Holy Spirit.

This is the beginning of the "take over" of Jesus and His kingdom. He is first taking over the hearts of men. Then He will take over the physical realm and then all of the created order, right down to the dirt and the trees. Each will be tried in the face of pressure where our love is being refined. The fire of His love consumes everything that gets in the way.

In the same way that He refines us as individuals, He will do this with the globe. The fire of God is primarily internal today, but it will be global and even external in the future. We must yield to His supernatural, internal fire today and agree with His heart to remove all that hinders this love in order to fulfill our primary life purpose, which is love itself. We want to be one with that flame and not be found resisting Him or in conflict with Him. We want to love what He loves and hate what He hates. We want a deep fiery affection for Him that agrees so definitely with

His heart that we are in the center of the storm, held close to Him, in the midst of shaking.

This fire of love that is so demanding in our personal lives is equally demanding in the earth. He wants us *all*, and He wants the created order too. He wants the kingdom to spread from the hearts of men to the earth. The fire of God that is being poured into our hearts today will enable us to not only remain faithful to the end, through the fire of tribulation, but it will also enable us to bring a multitude into the fellowship of His heart before and during the days of shaking. We will be burning and shining lamps in the darkest hour of human history if we remain in the fire of His love through agreeing with His heart. Our agreement with Him comes by warring against our sin and remaining in the vine by continuous conversation with Him through His Word. Even in our weakness we know His heart of mercy and run to Him again and again. We feel His deep desire for us and stand in His counsel by marking and perceiving His Word (Jer. 23:18). John the Baptist also stood and listened (John 3:29), and when He heard the voice of the Bridegroom, his joy was full. He spoke of judgment, and he had joy that was full because he heard the voice of love and desire.

Oh! There is no greater way to live. We are not of this world, but we are missionaries and ambassadors. We are friends of the Bridegroom beckoning all to come to the wedding. We have seen the end of the story, and we have heard His voice with personal, living understanding. Now we lift up our voices in the middle of the darkest night and cry, "Come! Come to the wedding." (See Matthew 22:4–5.) In the midnight hour we are calling people to come behold the Bridegroom (Matt. 25:6). We are persuading men to love Him. We give our lives to bring people to Him and cause them to see Him and love Him as He loves them.

The end-time church will be victorious in love: "Who is this coming up from the wilderness, leaning upon her beloved?" (Song of Sol. 8:5). The bride is leaning upon Jesus as her Beloved, empowered by love and gratitude. The church ends natural history with a leaning and loving heart as she is victorious in love. The Spirit prophetically speaks as He declares the bride's victory in the end times as she walks in love in the face of testing, temptations, and difficulties (Rev. 15:2). The church will be filled with glory and without compromise (Eph. 5:27), and Jesus's wife will be made ready (Rev. 19:7–8). Truly this is the most profound and grand story we have ever heard, and it will not fail. It is God's story, and every detail will come to pass.

CONCLUSION

Jesus knows the end of the story. He can see where we are going a billion years from now. When all we see in our personal lives is weak love, He sees real love. In the same way that He predicts where the seed of sin would lead, He also sees the seed of righteousness and sees the stunning tree that will blossom and take deep root for those who stay with it. He sees the end from the beginning (Isa. 46:10).

Many times throughout my life I have heard amazing, inspiring messages of wholeheartedness and abandonment. I have been to many altar calls to sign up to be one of these people of understanding and have felt the stirrings of being a messenger to prepare the way of Jesus's return. I have walked out of many meetings or read many books and sermons that inspire profound vision that has shaped me. But the thing that shocked me was how easily I strayed— sometimes even the next day. I was shocked when I first began to see this, but He was not shocked.

One of the most beautiful things about this whole story is that He chose weak and broken people to partner with, and He will not bring about this grand purpose without us. It is amazing. Yet I often felt like I could never attain, that I would never be strong enough to be a forerunner or devoted enough for such a grand picture, but over and over through the years He continually says to me, "I love you. You love Me. I know you do. Take it one day at a time. Just keep fighting. Stay in the race."

I want to give Him what He wants because it is my primary life purpose to satisfy His desire and to be His and partner with Him for eternity. I want to be His prize. At the end of my life I want to say, "I did it! I didn't give up! I didn't give in. I didn't draw back in shame, though I failed a thousand times. I didn't give up in doubt, though

I could not see You. I didn't quit when I was tired, but I pressed toward the prize. I did it! Here is what You wanted from me. Here is what You died for. Here is what You will fight for. Here is what I was created to be. Here is my heart! I am Yours! All Yours! In the dark night of faith I didn't draw back. I love You, Jesus! I love You, Jesus!"

Much of my walk with the Lord is a reach to love, but I want my heart to truly be moved by Him and toward Him where I not only reach for affection, but I also feel it. I want to take the reins of my mind and the reins of my soul, bringing them into agreement with Him, knowing that He calls it love every time I choose. When He sees me there struggling to sit in silence, trying to pray, living in secret, choosing righteousness when my lust pulls me in a different direction or when my pride wants to defend myself, but I restrain because I know He is watching, He says, "That's love."

I keep stoking the flame of love by every little choice I make, and one day I will have a bonfire. He sees the struggle. He sees the fight. He sees that I failed many times but got back and ran to Him instead of away from Him. He says, "That's love."

All of the shaking He is doing is about producing love in the hearts of all mankind. It comes through shaking and through understanding and seeing Him. I want to look Him in the eye on that day and present my heart to Him knowing it is the primary thing He was after the whole time. My entire life purpose is wrapped up in the day I stand before Him. I am measured by the size of my heart, and so is all of humanity. This whole thing is about love. Divine love, eternal, immortal, stronger than death. Love from eternity past. It is the fire in His eyes that will bring this love forth in me and bring it forth in the earth. He will do whatever it takes to fill the earth with the fire of His love, and nothing will get in His way, nothing will stop this fire, and nothing will hinder His purpose.

We are not aimless or without meaning. We are not spinning around on the earth in the midst of all the galaxies like a tiny aimless rock in the midst of a billion. We are not hopeless or without vision. We are caught up in His story. This whole thing is about Him. Every minute counts. Every deed done and every thought we think counts, because He is watching and we move Him deeply. Our lives are profoundly significant, and His love will bring us forth into the fullness of purpose and meaning. He will not relent until He has it all. He will not relent, and this is where our confidence lies. It is in the fire in His eyes.

To the end!

NOTES

Chapter Two
What Is God Looking For?

1. Viktor Frankl, *Man's Search for Ultimate Meaning* (New York: Basic Books, 2000).

Chapter Five
The Inside-Out, Upside-Down Kingdom

1. Mike Bickle, "Loving Jesus: The First Commandment Restored to First Place," http://mikebickle.org/resources/resource/3334 (accessed August 7, 2012).

2. Corrie Ten Boom with Elizabeth and John Sherrill, *The Hiding Place* (Grand Rapids, MI: Chosen, 2006), 216. Viewed at Google Books.

3. *The Hiding Place*, directed by James F. Collier (1975, Los Angeles: 20th Century Fox, 2006), DVD, as quoted in Phyllis Kirchberg, *The Profound Mystery: Marriage—the First Church* (New York: Vantage Press, 2008), 115. Viewed at Google Books.

4. Ibid.

Chapter Six
Fire of Love: Sustained by God

1. "Garden" by Misty Edwards. Copyright © 2007 by Forerunner Music. Used with permission.

2. Mike Bickle, *Harp and Bowl Handbook*, part 1, http://www.mikebickle.org.edgesuite.net/MikeBickleVOD/2008/Key_Apostolic_Intcessory_Prayers.pdf (accessed July 6, 2012).

CHAPTER NINE
THE END OF THE STORY

1. "Break the Chains" by Misty Edwards. Copyright © 2003 by Forerunner Music. Permission requested.

2. Wycliffe, *Annual Report 2010 Year in Review*, http://www.wycliffe.org/documents/corp_pub_2016_2010%20Annual%20Report%20-viewable-%20FINAL%20Low%20res.pdf (accessed July 6, 2012).